WHEN a young Ron Hill a1 Hee were forced to take ₜₑₘₚₒᵣₐᵣy ₛₕₑₗₜₑᵣ ᵢₙ ₜₕₑ port of Weymouth in 1937 during a stormy voyage from the Channel Islands to Plymouth, he did not imagine then that he would ever return to the little harbour in Dorset. However, as the dark clouds of World War 2 were gathering in 1939, that earlier chance visit was to seal his fate. Army officials were seeking a boat capable of carrying soldiers and ammunition to the Breakwater Forts guarding the naval base at Portland, and a skipper who knew the seas around the area. Ron and his larger vessel *My Girl* met their needs. *My Girl* was requisitioned for duties and thus it was that Ron returned to Weymouth.

This book is the story of *My Girl*, the pleasure boat that went to war, and is a thrilling first-hand history of the war years as experienced locally, including the build up to D-Day and beyond, when American troops departed from Weymouth and Portland bound for Omaha Beach in Normandy.

NB: The cover photograph shows bombs being dropped over the Chequered Fort on Portland Harbour Breakwater during World War 2, and the small jetty where 'My Girl' landed troops, stores and shells for the guns of the fort.

Ron Hill, skipper of *My Girl*, pictured shortly after his posting to Weymouth for war service in 1939.
(Author's Collection)

WEYMOUTH AT WAR

Ron Hill's story of the vessel *My Girl* as told to Marian Lye

Wee Hee (in foreground) stormbound in Weymouth Harbour 1937 after her voyage from the Channel Islands.

Published by
Filament Publishing Ltd
16 Croydon Road, Waddon, Croydon,
Surrey, CR0 4PA, United Kingdom
+44 (0)20 8688 2598
www.filamentpublishing.com

ISBN 978-1-910819-77-7

First edition published in 1990 by Dorset Publishing Company
at the Wincanton Press, Somerset.
Text by Ron Hill as told to Marian Lye

Cover photo courtesy of Geoffrey Carter.

The poems *Sea Fever* and *Consecration*
by John Masefield are reproduced by kind permission
of the Society of Authors.

Table of Contents

Key to the chart - figures relate to Weymouth and Portland Breakwaters and Harbour Installations.

I	Northern Arm Breakwater.
2	Bincleaves Torpedo Range Jetty.
3	Carpenters Store and Crane.
4	R.N. Torpedo Long Range and Jetty.
5	Northern Arm Landing Steps. Outside and inside.
6	C. Pier Head. Outside and inside landings.
7	Middle Arm Breakwater.
8	B. Pier Head. Landing steps inside.
9	Whiteheads Torpedo Range. Outer landings.
10	A. Pier Head Lighthouse. Landing steps inside and outside.
11	Breakwater Fort (Chequered) Camber. Landing inside.
12	Outer Arm Breakwater.
13	D. Head. Entrance blocked by H.M.S. *Hood.* 1914.
14	Dockyard Camber Jetty.
15	Admiralty Torpedo Range.
16	H.M.S. *Foylebank* attacked and sunk.
17	H.M.S. *Himalaya* attacked and sunk.
18	*Hartlepool.* Freighter, sunk.
19	*Alex van Opstal,* mined and sunk.
20	Boom Defences.

Sketch map of Weymouth and Portland

See opposite page for key to numbers

north

one mile

Redcliff Point

Ringstead Bay

Whitenose

WEYMOUTH

18

Weymouth Harbour

Nothe Fort

Bincleaves

North Entrance

WEYMOUTH BAY

Whitehead Torpedo Factory

Torpedo Range

PORTLAND HARBOUR

East Entrance

CASTLETOWN

South Entrance (blocked by HMS Hood)

WEST BAY

VERNE

Grove Point

Blacknor Point

PORTLAND

Lightship

PORTLAND BILL

Lighthouse

The Race

The Shambles

Compilation: D. Hill
Drawing: Christopher Fudge

7

My Girl at Hope Quay with crew members Cyril Johnson and Nelson Smith. The frame attached to the mast carries identification lights which had to be shown by vessels during the war. (Author's Collection)

Introduction

One of the most familiar sights in Weymouth in summertime is the pleasure boat *My Girl*, either tied up at her jetty, or setting out across the bay with carefree holidaymakers aboard, bound for Portland Harbour. As Weymouth has been her home since 1939, some residents can recall that she had an honourable record of service in World War 2, but know little of the details.

Here is the story of *My Girl* – the pleasure boat that went to war. Her skipper in wartime and peace, Ron Hill, recounted his memories to his daughter, the writer Marian Lye, and here is his personal record, in words and pictures, of Weymouth at War from 1939 to 1945. Throughout that time, *My Girl*, in the service of the War Department, sailed continually between Weymouth and Portland and the Breakwater Forts of Portland Harbour, often under aerial bombardment. Come fair weather or foul, *My Girl* was on-duty, carrying officers, soldiers and doctors, ENSA concert parties and the eagerly awaited mail from sweethearts and families.

Despite the dangers of bombing, mines and stormy weather, she carried without a single loss thousands of forces members to and from the forts, together with consignments of 50 half-hundredweight shells for the big guns, and 500 gallon loads of paraffin then used in the operation of the anti-aircraft

Ron Hill aboard *My Girl* at Hope Quay, preparing for another day's duties conveying men and stores to the Portland Breakwater Forts. (Author's Collection)

searchlights. She also helped to embark at Weymouth part of the huge D-Day army of American troops bound for the Normandy beaches, to begin the liberation of Europe.

This is the story of courage and endurance amid great turmoil, of hope for the future, and of love — for two special ladies, Dolores and *My Girl*.

Marian commences the book with her recollections of growing up with 'My Girl' during the 1950s. Her words convey just how much this vessel was loved and regarded as part of the family. Then, in 'Stormbound at Weymouth', she takes us further back in time to begin her father's story, with his first chance visit to Weymouth in 1937: a visit that sealed his destiny and returned him there in 1939, as the Clouds of War were looming.....

Winter morning. Commencing duties at Hope Quay.

Three of the children of Ron and Dolores at Bowleaze Cove,
Weymouth in 1949. Left to right: Ron, Marian and Julia.
(Author's Collection)

The children of Ron and Dolores Hill, pictured in 1955.
Left to right: Marian, Ron, John, Julia and Christopher.
(Author's Collection)

Growing up with *My Girl*

It was easy to tell that we were children from a seafaring background; as well as being able to recite our multiplication tables, we could reel off all the shipping forecast areas! Without exception, each day in our household began and ended with the BBC Shipping Forecast, and we paid full attention whenever "Wight, Portland, Plymouth" were mentioned. Our lives hinged on the rise and fall of the barometer, the wind and the tide. At any time of the day or night, be it Christmas or other high days or holidays, if there were storms or unusually high tides, Ron went down to the harbour to see if *My Girl* was holding safe on her moorings, or needed pumping out. *My Girl* was his livelihood and she was part of the family; we loved her, and our years revolved around her.

Soon after the war ended, Weymouth came into its own again as a seaside holiday resort. Summer was the best of times, and saw the town fill with holidaymakers and day trippers, all happy and excited to be taking a break from their everyday lives. *My Girl* resumed her role as a pleasure boat and we enjoyed sun-filled days on the beach close to her base, swimming and sharing picnic lunches packed by our mother, Dolores. My brothers spent much of their time then helping out on board, assisting passengers, and watching the mooring ropes and the pontoons. If there were spaces left, my sister and I loved to go along on a trip with Ron.

Sometimes, on a summer day, easterly winds would send too much surf onto the beach for the boats to run, or during a voyage, dense fog would roll in across the sea, blotting out everything in sight and muffling sounds. With a crewman keeping a lookout in the bow, and the klaxon sounding regularly, Ron would navigate by compass to steer *My Girl* safely back to base.

The summer seasons flew by all too quickly, however, and during the winter months, Ron set lobster pots and trawled for fish aboard the *Wee Hee* to make ends meet, selling his catch at Hanney Brothers, the fish wholesalers in Weymouth. He was often at sea in poor weather conditions, and we were always relieved when he returned, tired but safe, at the end of his fishing trips. When money was in very short supply, if we children needed new shoes and *My Girl* needed new engine parts, there was never any contest; we knew the boat had to come first. I also recall that we did eat a lot of fish in those days!

As each winter gave way to spring, Dolores packed more picnic lunches at weekends, and we clambered aboard *My Girl*, either on her moorings or on the slipway, to help with the process of cleaning and repainting to prepare her for the coming summer. We all learned to sandpaper the woodwork with the grain of the timber, and became adept in the techniques needed to apply marine varnish and gloss paint.

The boys also helped to strip and rebuild the engine, and mastered the art of making rope fenders, while Dolores sewed new canvas covers for the cork lifebelts and repainted *My Girl*'s beautiful name boards every year. Time and energy were never spared, or begrudged, to ensure she looked her very best for each new holiday season.

Dolores was a star. She kept the home going, took care of all the boat's accounts and tax returns, and ensured crew members were paid. There were many occasions when she had to pick her way from the back door to the washing line via lobster pots stacked up in the backyard awaiting a coat of tar, or cope with a live lobster or several newly caught fish flapping around in her kitchen sink, ready for cleaning and cooking. She was always knitting fishermen's sweaters or long white socks for Ron's sea boots, along with pullovers and socks for my brothers.

Mealtimes were often delayed, especially if the weather deteriorated suddenly or Ron responded to the maroons sent skywards from the Lifeboat Station. One entire wardrobe in the boys' room was taken over by charts, books, oilskins, signal flags and sea boots. This was not too much of a hardship for my brothers, however, as we had just three sets of clothes each then; one to wash, one to wear, and one to spare! In addition to the store which Ron had close to Hope Square, half of the kitchen cupboards were used for the storage of ropes, boat bits and tins of paint or varnish.

My Girl, proudly flying the Royal Artillery Association pennant awarded in 1994. (Courtesy of Keith Pritchard, Marine Journalist)

Whenever Ron repainted all the kitchen cupboard doors, Dolores could have any colour she liked – as long as it was cabin roof blue, hull white, or waterline red!

Our early years were amazing in so many ways. On clear winter nights, Ron would ensure we were clad in warm clothes to go outdoors to look up at the stars, and tell us their names and point out the constellations – vital knowledge for sailors and navigators. He taught us the points of the compass, read stories to us, and sang for us some of the sea shanties he had learned from his father. Above all, he instilled in us his love and respect for the sea, and an awareness that the sea seldom gives second chances.

Today, even a fleeting glimpse of *My Girl*, awaiting her passengers beside the Coastline Cruises kiosk at Brewers Quay, brings back all the special memories of our childhood days.

M.L

Rough Sea, Stone Pier, Weymouth.

Heavy seas crashing over the Stone Pier at the entrance to Weymouth Harbour. In storm conditions, with a full complement of men and stores, rounding the Stone Pier with *My Girl* was a hazardous and uncomfortable experience.
(Courtesy Weymouth Museum)

Stormbound at Weymouth

Fate delivered me to the port of Weymouth for the first time in September 1937, when more dead than alive after a frightening ordeal at sea, I sought shelter there from the gales raging in the Channel.

What began as an outing to Torquay Regatta with two friends – I was 22 and they were about the same age – had turned on impulse to a voyage to the Channel Islands that almost ended in disaster. As I tied up my small craft alongside the boats moored near Town Bridge, I never imagined this unexpected visit was going to change the whole course of my life. In the event it was to result in my return less that two years later as the clouds of war were gathering over Britain.

My story begins in Plymouth, where the summer of 1937 had proved to be a very successful season for my brother and me, running Father's recently acquired pleasure boat *Irene*, licensed to carry 26 passengers, from the Promenade Pier. The worst of the Great Depression was over and folk began to enjoy their leisure time again, with trips to the seaside being eagerly anticipated events. Trains and coaches brought vast numbers of people to the West Country, and a boat trip to see places of interest along the beautiful Devon coast and the warships at Devonport was the high spot of the holiday for many of them.

There was no time off for us during the summer, and we worked from dawn to dusk each day. Although the hours were long, life was good, for what could be better than sailing the sunlit sea with parties of people all intent on enjoying themselves? After years of struggling to gain a living from the erratic harvest of the sea, our entry into the pleasure boat trade had caused our family fortunes to take a decided turn for the better; there was even the prospect of the purchase of the newly built passenger launch *My Girl*, capable of carrying 66 people, for the next season.

Our new found success contrasted greatly with the poverty of our early years and the hardships endured by generations of mariners in the family before us. I was little more than a boy when I began trawling with my father during lonely days and nights in an open boat, and I went on to experience the dangers of life on the cable ships *John W. Mackay* and *Marie Louise Mackay*, which ventured into the far reaches of the Atlantic Ocean, laying the transatlantic telephone cables across the ocean floor. Although long and hard, my apprenticeship confirmed within me that the sea was the only calling I ever wanted to follow, and my love for it never wavered. However, there were times when Father Neptune tested me to within an inch of my life, and September 1937 was to provide such a challenge.

As the summer trade dwindled to a halt, I met up with my friend Billy Colleyhoe and his mate John at the Plymouth

Boxing Club where I did a bit of competitive boxing and also went for training. Billy and John were on a week's holiday from their jobs, and as both were keen anglers, they usually spent their weekends and holidays camping near the coast at Bigbury Bay or Yealm Point, where they fished from the rocks for pollack and bass.

We got talking and it was suggested that we all go to Torquay for a few days, as it was Regatta Week. Although they were not used to the sea as I was, they thought it would be a good idea to go by boat, so plans were made and I asked Father's permission to take our fishing boat, *Wee Hee*. This was given with some reluctance, despite the fact that I had worked non-stop all the year, and deserved a break.

Wee Hee – named after the local word for a sea swallow or tern – was a 21 ft. Mevagissey Tosher, and we set to work to equip her for our trip. Billy's camping gear was put aboard, the main item being a six foot ridge tent which we would be able to spread over the gaff and tie to the gunwales to provide shelter for sleeping when we were in harbour. A primus stove, mugs, cooking pot and kettle, and a large can of water completed our needs. There was no necessity to stock up with food as we could go ashore at Torquay for meals, but we took a packet of Quaker Oats for our breakfast. Billy brought his Brownie box camera to record the highlights of the Regatta.

I checked the fuel for the boat and fixed a compass to a seat on the port side. This was not a good idea as it would not give a true course, but we did not intend to go far.

At 4 p.m. we were ready to go. I was familiar with the coastline and the first part of our trip was uneventful; past Yealm Head, Bolt Tail and Bolt Head, Prawle Point and on to Start Point. It was then that Billy suggested a change of plan: "Let's go to the Channel Islands!"

John immediately fell in with the idea, but I had no navigation lights or charts to plot a course, and I wasn't for the venture at all. I had never been to the islands, although I knew their position off the French coast. It was now about 9 p.m. and very dark, with heavy clouds scudding across the sky. Nothing was going to deter my companions, however.

"It's not much further than Torquay," they argued. "We'll be back before anyone knows we've gone."

There was a good sailing breeze and I set a south-east course by the compass. The *Wee Hee* had a 3.5 horsepower engine which was economical on fuel, but we would have to use sail as much as possible. We were well out in the Channel, and having to keep a good lookout in the darkness, when suddenly, lights from a freighter appeared as if from nowhere and she was bearing straight down upon us. I had only a hand torch, with which I signalled frantically, but it was a desperate moment. I took a round turn with the boat and just got clear in time, but we were left wallowing in the freighter's wake. I realised my stupidity in starting on this voyage. Billy and John, however, were full of the spirit of adventure – and adventure was certainly what we got.

We continued across the Channel during the night, and towards dawn we picked up a flashing signal which proved to be Les Hanois on the south-west coast of Guernsey. When daylight came, I saw to my horror that we were nearing a coast so rocky that I feared the boat would be holed at any minute. There was no harbour to be seen, and my only thought was to get away from those treacherous rocks, so I set sail to go northward, hoping to come down the east coast and make St Peter Port. The weather was now full of sudden squalls, and continuous pumping out was necessary. I sighted a small French fishing boat with a single hand aboard and hailed him to ask direction for St Peter Port. He seemed not to understand at first, but presently he took in his gear and beckoned me to follow him. The Frenchman guided us expertly through the rocks, and before he turned into St Sampson's Harbour, he indicated that we should continue a little further south. Soon I was able to see the Cross Channel boats and knew we had gained St Peter Port. We entered harbour and went alongside the camber, whereupon the pilot came over to us from his hut on the breakwater and enquired our business.

On learning that we were from Plymouth and were hoping to get back there, he could hardly credit that we had come that distance in such a small craft.

"Don't you try to get back in this bad weather," he warned. "You'll have to get the boat shipped back to Weymouth on the Channel Island steamer."

But we didn't have the money to do that. The pilot directed us to moor alongside a small yacht named Onyx, and Billy and John disappeared into the town. I went ashore to send a telegram home, but returned to the boat as soon as I could. By evening the weather had worsened and the Pilot told us we could sleep that night in the *Onyx*, which had been stripped of her interior furnishings and left in his care prior to laying up for the winter. It was bitterly cold aboard, and I couldn't sleep a wink as I tried to plan our next move. The days would soon go by, and my companions had to be back in Plymouth to go to work. As for me, quite apart from wanting to ease my mother's worries, I was dreading the reception I would get from Father, and I was determined to get that particular ordeal over as quickly as possible.

As daylight approached, the weather had improved slightly, and with clear skies, we were able to see the coast of Alderney some 20 miles to the north-east. We decided to make it to Alderney, and from there start our homeward journey. The pilot was quite horrified by this idea, and drew our attention to the dangerous tidal race known as The Swinge, which had claimed many vessels, together with the damaged, partly submerged breakwater and treacherous outlying rocks.

Nevertheless, as the weather had considerably brightened by mid-morning, we decided to attempt the journey.

We had gone only a few miles when we were overtaken by heavy squalls. However, there was nothing for it but to carry on, and it was nearly sunset when we gained the shelter of Braye Harbour, where we tied up alongside a small fishing boat moored inside the jetty. Three French fishing boats from Camaret were already sheltering inside the harbour. These were sturdy vessels noted for their seaworthiness and they each carried a crew of about four.

Billy and John climbed the ladder on to the breakwater and made off in search of food, returning some three hours later to tell me how they had enjoyed fried mackerel and chips served from the open window of a cottage. We tried to settle down for the night under our makeshift tent shelter, but I found it impossible to sleep. During a break in the clouds, a full moon shone out, and as I glanced over the side of the boat to check the depth of water beneath us, I discovered that we were almost touching the bottom. The tide had fallen some 36 feet. At home in Plymouth, the greatest tide fall would have been about 14 and a half feet.

The next day, we decided to start our journey back to Plymouth, and although I knew the voyage would be a hard one, I did not visualise the nightmare that we were about to be plunged into.

Before leaving Alderney, I reefed the foresail and the mainsail, and unshipped the mizzenmast, stowing it on the afterdeck of the *Wee Hee*. At 8 a.m. we were under way. Using the engine and the minimum of sail, we passed through the infamous Swinge and negotiated the Ortec Channel. As we approached the Casquets, the south-westerly wind was gathering strength, causing the seas to pile up around us, and holding the main sheet with one hand and the tiller with the other, I struggled to steer a north-westerly course towards Start Point.

An hour and a half out from the Casquets, we ran into the worst weather imaginable. We were now in the Hurd Deep, a channel some 80 fathoms deep in places. The wind had reached gale force and was screaming about our ears as we held on for our lives on a grim roller coaster ride over the waves. Mountains of water loomed over us, lifted us and then sent us hurtling down into deep, dark chasms, causing us to fear that the bow of the *Wee Hee* would never rise towards the skies again. Then a huge white-capped wave crashed over us, washing the floorboards from under our feet and putting the engine out of action. We were left gasping for breath and drenched to the skin. Our situation was truly horrific, for we had half a ton of iron ballast in the bilges, no bouyancy apparatus and no life jackets. One more big sea aboard would sink us like a stone.

"Keep pumping! Keep pumping!" I shouted to the others as I held the tiller and bailed frantically at the same time, desperately running with the wind and the heavy seas. God, how could I have been so foolish in being influenced to make this journey against my better judgement and experience! But this was no time for self-recrimination – all our lives were at stake, and I just had to keep the boat afloat until we reached safety.

We battled on through the storm and eventually sighted a steamer in the distance, probably making for Guernsey from Southampton. She was visible one minute, then vanished the next as the waves reared up between us, but it was somehow reassuring that we were not alone on those terrible seas. As heavy squalls continued to lash us, lightning flashed across the western sky. Soon darkness would fall and we were completely at the mercy of the elements. All at once, there was a glimpse of the setting sun, whose red glow was reflected from the sails of a four-masted ship travelling up Channel. In an instant, she disappeared; it was as if we had seen a mirage. That strange vision gave me hope, for I realised that she was probably a Swedish vessel, one of Erikson's fleet, returning from Australia en route for London to discharge her cargo of grain or wool. She would certainly have called at Falmouth, so we were more than halfway back across the Channel.

I managed to coax the engine of the *Wee Hee* back into life, and some hours later we saw a light on our port side, which we supposed was Start Point.

After passing through very rough, broken water, we at last sighted land. Visibility was poor, with torrents of rain, but I was sure this was not Start Point, for the contour of this land rose higher to the eastward, whereas Start Point rose higher to westward. I wondered how far we had been driven off course. Could this be Portland, near the little seaside resort of Weymouth?

"Look!" Billy exclaimed. 'There's a light over there, and an entrance to a harbour. Come on, let's go in!"

In the darkness and lashing rain, I made for the entrance, but I suddenly saw a mass of white water breaking across the opening and a red light strung on to cables above. I pushed hard down on the tiller and jibbed over on to the other tack, just in time. That opening had been blocked in the 1914-18 war with the old battleship HMS *Hood* to prevent entry by German submarines. Our mast would have been ripped out by the cables and the boat wrecked on the *Hood* had I not realised the danger hidden there.

I followed the line of the breakwater for about a mile and could just see the glow of a town ahead, so I steered in that direction, for there would surely be a harbour nearby. Soon I realised we were coming close to shore, as the sea was now breaking into white rollers. I took a turn to port and could just make out some buildings and a pier.

A man on the pier shouted directions and we were soon safely inside Weymouth Harbour. Within minutes of our arrival, a Customs officer appeared on the quayside, demanding to know from whence we had come.

"We're from the Channel Islands!" I shouted. "From Alderney!"

At first, the officer could not believe that a craft the size of ours had come across the Channel on such a night, and he ordered me to go up harbour and tie up just below the Town Bridge. This I did, and two Customs officers were soon aboard. They now seemed convinced that we had indeed come from the Channel Islands, and they proceeded to make a thorough search of the boat, ripping up floorboards and throwing out the contents of the lockers, including our bits of dry clothes. Everything was strewn around in the pouring rain. Needless to say, they found no contraband.

It was well past midnight. The officers became aware of the fact that we were all dead beat, hungry and soaking wet, but lucky to be alive. The Seamen's Mission, which only opened after ten o'clock at night for shipwrecked mariners, was contacted and the couple in charge were very kind to us. A large stove in the kitchen was banked up to dry our wet clothes, we had mugs of hot tea and some biscuits, and were each allocated a small cubicle where we could at last get some real sleep.

The next morning, we returned to the boat fully expecting that we could continue our journey back to Plymouth. The yacht to which we had tied up was the *Majestic*, which I recognised as a former herring drifter that had often called into Plymouth before her conversion to a yacht. Her owner, Mr W. Underwood, came on deck and talked with us, and persuaded us to stay another day at least, since the gales had in no way abated. Billy took his camera over to the other side of the harbour and took a photograph of the *Wee Hee* with John and me aboard. They then went into the town to look around and we spent another night at the Mission.

The following morning, a Saturday, we again considered leaving for home. Mr Underwood told us of the great danger in rounding Portland Bill, where the Race was the worst hazard of all the South Coast. There would be no hope for a small vessel like ours, once drawn into that boiling cauldron. His skipper, Bill Mann, offered to take me on the back of his motorbike to see for myself what conditions were like at Portland Bill. Bill Mann hailed from Exmouth where his father was coxswain of the lifeboat, but he had his own fishing boat at Weymouth, the *Water Witch*. She had a crew of two and was used for trawling and scallop dredging.

My journey on Bill Mann's motorbike over the nine miles between the Town Bridge and Portland Bill was a new experience for me, and nearly as frightening as my sea adventure. The machine had no pillion seat – I sat astride the metal carrier – and there were no footrests either, so this meant that I had to hang on tightly as we climbed the steep road to reach the top of the island. On arriving at the Bill and seeing the turmoil of the waters of the Race before me, I was thankful that I had not set out to try to sail through that maelstrom.

The keeper of the Portland Lighthouse invited me to the top of the tower to get a better view of the extent of the Race both up and down the Channel. The scene from the tower was fantastic, for the sea was awesome in its anger. Everywhere great mountains of white water hurled themselves at each other, and clouds of spray rose into the air like steam released from pressure. Wind and tide seemed to be wrestling to change the location and extent of their battleground. Small ships would be swallowed by those seas within seconds and their bones thrown upon the rocks of Portland Headland, or ground down on the shingle banks guarded by the nearby Shambles Lightship. This was a truly terrible place, to be avoided at all costs.

I began to despair of getting back home. However, the lighthouse keeper suggested that I call on Vic Charles, who lived in a coastguard cottage near the tower. Vic had a lifetime's experience of tides and weather conditions at the Bill. Before he could do any fishing, his own boat had to be lowered into the sea from Godnor Point by one of the old wooden cranes belonging to the stone firms.

Vic was making up some potting gear but came over to us and asked what we wanted. On hearing my story and of my intention to get back to Plymouth, he strongly advised against attempting to round the Bill. I told him I had come through the dreadful Swinge off Alderney and survived the perils of Hurd Deep. Was there no safe channel inside the Race of which he could advise me? Vic fell silent. It was as if he were sizing me up. Then he seemed satisfied.

"Look, Ron," he said. "There's an area of calmer water between the Bill and the Race, but it's only safe to try at slack water. You must keep in as close as possible, watching out for dangerous rocks." Gradually, a plan was devised. "Bring your boat round from Weymouth, to be at the Bill by 7 o'clock tomorrow morning. I'll be on Godnor Point, so watch me carefully. If on seeing you I walk steadily toward the Bill without stopping or looking back, you'll know it's safe to round the Bill. However, if I turn and wave you back to Weymouth, mind you get back as fast as you can."

With Vic's instructions firmly in my mind, I rode pillion back to Weymouth to make plans for an early start next morning. The distance by sea from Weymouth to Portland is about 7 miles, so we left just after 5 a.m. to arrive at the Bill by 7 o'clock. Nearing Godnor Point, I could see Vic on the cliff. He acknowledged me and started walking deliberately towards the Bill. Without once looking back, he continued walking and I knew we could proceed carefully on our way. Remembering his precise words, I kept in fairly close, watching for any rocks lying just beneath the surface. There was a ground swell and we were pitching into it. Although the sails were useless head on to the wind, I kept them hoisted, the sheets pulled flat aft, just in case the engine failed or the propeller got fouled.

The eddy was slowly pulling us around the Bill past Pulpit Rock. Not far off the Race was still boiling, but we had succeeded. I could now breathe easily again. I had proved Vic's trust in me, for had we met with disaster, he would have held himself responsible. Safely around the Bill, we could now set course for Berry Head and Start Point. The wind was still a strong south-westerly and would be against us for some 49 miles. Because visibility was poor, with some heavy showers, a constant lookout was necessary. About an hour out of Portland, we sighted a sailing vessel heading westward. She was dipping low into the water and a man who was on the bowsprit, rigging the jib, was getting pretty wet. With her sails set, she changed course seaward and we lost sight of her. I reckoned later that she was probably from Dartmouth Royal Naval College, with trainee cadets aboard. We continued with sail and engine all through the afternoon and picked up the Berry Head light at about 5.30 p.m.

I knew we were on course and would soon approach the waters and headlands with which I was familiar. We passed Berry Head, keeping some distance off, then Dartmouth and across Start Bay. There was vivid lightning followed by heavy rumbles of thunder and the tide was flowing up Channel again. I warned Billy and John that I would be keeping inshore to get more shelter, so they must keep a good lookout. After so many long hours, there was a danger that tiredness would make them less vigilant.

At 9 p.m. or thereabouts, we picked up Start Point Light and continued westward, arriving off Yealm Head at about 11.30 p.m. On we went to the Mewstone and then we opened up the Breakwater Light. My spirits rose, for we would soon be in calmer water. I headed for the Eastern Channel of the Plymouth Breakwater, through the Cattewater into Sutton Harbour and our moorings at Guy's Quay. We were home at last. Billy and John lost no time in gathering their gear together and getting off home. I lowered sail, lifted the keel, pumped out, put out the support "legs" aside the boat to prevent grounding, and then, in some dread, made my way home. It was now after 2 a.m.

The door was locked. I knocked. No reply. I knocked again. There was some movement now and Father's voice called: "Who is it?"

"Ron!"

"Where's the boat?"

"She's on the moorings."

"Is she all right?"

"Yes, she's all right!"

Only then was the door unlocked and I was allowed in. On seeing me, Father must have guessed that I had been having a hard time and he didn't ask any more questions, but merely told me to get a cup of tea and go to bed, as he wanted me up at 6 a.m. to prepare the *Irene* for the day's work. I turned in, truly thankful that the nightmare voyage was over.

Early in the morning, I went down to the quay to get the *Irene* ready and we were off to the Promenade Pier by 8 o'clock. The recently completed *Queen Mary*, the largest liner in the world at that time, had anchored in Cawsand Bay and people came flocking into the boats to go to see her. I was back at work, still exhausted after my adventure, but so glad to be alive.

The stern discipline of the sea had taught me an important lesson, for I vowed that never again would I allow anyone to influence me against my better judgement. I realise to this day how fortunate I was to survive that risky voyage across the Channel. It brings to mind an old phrase, often used by

Devonshire folk when concluding expressions of their hopes and plans: "... if the Lord spares." Those who venture upon the oceans are constantly reminded of their vulnerability in confronting the elements, for the sea seldom gives second chances.

I still have the original photographs of Braye Harbour and Weymouth Harbour taken during that trip, together with a Certificate of Pratique given to me by the Customs at Weymouth, dated 16 September 1937. On the day the certificate was issued, I did not dream that fate was soon to return me to Weymouth as a consequence of that very voyage.

Note:

Plymouth has long provided a welcome landfall for sailors completing more illustrious voyages than mine. I chanced upon one such adventurer in 1935 when I assisted the owner of the little yacht *Emanuel* as she limped into port. Her owner, Commander R.D. Graham, had just returned across the Atlantic, having made an epic single-handed voyage from England to the New World in 1934. His crossing and his travels down the Eastern Seaboard to Bermuda later featured in his book *Rough Passage*.

Having landed a passenger in Plymouth at the end of his return journey, Commander Graham was heading for home when he was caught in a fierce squall off Bolt Head, near Salcombe. The stay wires on the port side of the boat had all snapped and he had great difficulty in manoeuvring his vessel. He asked me if I could recommend anyone who could splice in the stay wires and put the yacht ashore to clear the weed which had accumulated on her hull during the long voyage. I fetched my father and it was agreed that we would undertake the work while the Commander travelled home by train for a few days' rest. He invited us to read the log he had kept during his voyage, and to finish up a box of oranges still on board.

On his return to Plymouth, the Commander was very pleased with all the work that Father and I had done on the yacht. Whilst Father and he were yarning together, it suddenly became apparent that they had both been aboard the old battleship HMS *Jupiter* when she was iced in at Archangel while on convoy duties to Russia during the First World War.

The ship was unable to escape for six months and when food and water ran out, her crew had to survive by hunting seals for meat and melting ice for drinking water.

Commander Graham had been Chief Navigating Officer on the ship at the time, while father was an able seaman, so their paths never crossed on board. However, once that link had been established, they had plenty of tales to catch up on, and both had silver medals presented to them by Nicholas II, the last Tsar of Russia.

Old Mevagissey

My Girl was built in Mevagissey, and was named after the
hit musical *Me and My Girl*.
(Courtesy of Keith Pritchard, Marine Journalist)

The Clouds of War

The year 1938 was to prove to be our most successful ever as our newest and largest craft *My Girl*, a 36 ft. passenger launch able to carry 66 people, went into service. Built in Mitchell Brothers yard at Mevagissey, *My Girl* combined the very finest skills in design and boatbuilding available in Britain, and with her ten ft. six inch beam and three ft. draught, she was ideally suited to our particular work. She was fitted with a Kelvin Ricardo four cylinder 36 horsepower petrol/paraffin engine, and was duly licensed by the Board of Trade for the pleasure boat business, with myself as skipper and my younger brother Bert as engineer.

The acquisition of this beautiful vessel was the prize for which we had laboured so long. She was the pearl in the string of boats we owned, and the lustrous white paintwork of her hull showed off to perfection her strong, elegant lines. She was soundly and honestly built and moved as gracefully as a swan upon the surface of the water, whatever the elements chose to throw at her. Between *My Girl* and me, there grew a special bond that is hard to explain to anyone who has not been closely linked to the sea and ships. I understood her every mood, whim and response, and man and boat existed together in a trusting, harmonious partnership.

We were now able to book whole coachloads of holidaymakers for cruises along the historic shoreline of Plymouth, and there were private charter trips up the rivers Yealm and Tamar, passing wonderful scenery and pausing at little jetties near farm cottages where strawberries and cream teas were served. There were trips to Bovisand and Cawsand, taking coaches of people to enjoy the sunny hours on the beaches. Some even took camping equipment to Bovisand and pitched their tents on the adjoining fields to stay for the weekend. What happy days they were!

John Antonussi's son often travelled with us, taking ice cream from his father's parlour in Plymouth to sell on the beaches. Returning later in the evenings, our passengers would have a sing-song with guitar accompaniment by Antonussi and a young employee, John Morris. Passenger boats also paid an annual fee for permission to land passengers at Fort Bovisand, and often conveyed servicemen from Fort Bovisand to Plymouth, returning them at 10.30 p.m. after an evening's liberty. We were especially busy when visiting regiments of the Royal Artillery arrived at the fort to compete for the King's Cup, an annual shooting event. It seemed then that nothing could ever go wrong – we were riding on the crest of a wave after years of struggling to survive. The following year held the promise of another good season, and so it proved, until August came and the threat of war suddenly brought an ominous foreboding.

On 28 August 1939, as the clouds of war were gathering, enquiries were already being made as to what boats were suitable for requisition. Major A. Glass, the Royal Army Service Corps (RASC) Transport Officer at Cumberland Block, Devonport, was conducting the enquiry and wanted a vessel for service at Weymouth. He had been informed that I had been to Weymouth and knew the port, although in fact I had only been stormbound there briefly after the Channel Islands adventure. That one visit was to seal my fate, however, for Major Glass decided to requisition *My Girl*.

Our world was suddenly turned upside down. Bert and I were told that we could volunteer to go with *My Girl*, otherwise she would be put into the hands of the Army, and soldiers would run her. As we went home to talk things over, we were shocked and dispirited, for it was as if the cup of success had been dashed from our hands. We were given just three hours to make our decision, and we decided we would go with our boat. For my part, I knew I could not abandon her to strangers who might ill-use her. Father was of the opinion that even if war came, it would surely be all over by Christmas. Terms of Agreement were drawn up between Father and the Officer in Charge, Land and Water Transport, RASC South Western Area, and we were ordered to proceed to Weymouth with *My Girl* immediately.

T.691   S E C R E T

Gentlemen,

~~In confirmation of my telegram of today's date,~~
I am to acquaint you that the ~~s.s.~~/m.~~v.~~ *My Girl*,
being required for urgent Government service, is hereby
requisitioned on the conditions of the

enclosed { Pro-Forma Charter Party T.98
          { ~~Pro-Forma Charter Party T.99~~

        It is regretted that the exigencies of the case
preclude prior agreement of the rate of hire, but unless
otherwise arranged this matter will be determined by the
Tribunal to be constituted for the purpose.

        The following are enclosed for your information
and return, where necessary, to the undersigned:-

    T.620 Memorandum for the guidance of Owners.

    T.611A Particulars to enable date of entry into pay to
                    be settled.

    T.619 Particulars of Small Craft

    T.640 Notes on claims and accounts.

        A payment on account of hire will be made as
soon as possible after receipt of a claim.

        His Majesty's Government relies on the goodwill
of yourselves, your staff and agents in carrying out these
instructions and preparing the ship for the King's
service, especially as regards clearing cargo, fuelling,
storing and manning.

                        I am, Gentlemen,
                            Your obedient Servant,

                        Superintending Sea Transport
                            Officer *in charge*
                                Devonport

T.M.557/39

Requisition Document for *My Girl*, 1939.

Bert and I prepared *My Girl* for the voyage to Weymouth, taking aboard about 20 gallons of paraffin and two extra cans of petrol, while mother packed some food for us. We made our farewells to our parents and sister Doris, and departed from Plymouth at 4 p.m., leaving behind all that we held dear without knowing what the future held in store for us. War had not yet been declared, but there was little doubt in our hearts that it would come soon.

By the time we reached Start Point, darkness had fallen and thick fog was closing in. Rather than continue our journey steering by compass along a hazardous coastline which offered no safe harbour, I returned to Salcombe where we made our way upstream to anchor. We slept on the floorboards of our boat, under a canvas canopy, and with the fog persisting, it was bitterly cold. When daylight came, the fog lifted slightly and we continued on our way, once again reaching Start Point and continuing to Berry Head, where I branched east for Portland Bill, some 40 miles distant. I was soon able to make out Bridport and West Bay, and I had to steam out towards the Bill, as the wind was freshening from the south-west, driving us towards Chesil Beach. I did not care to contemplate our fate if we were thrown upon the Chesil Bank, where fingers of surf clawed at the beach and a treacherous undertow sucked noisily and greedily at the pebbles.

I was well aware of the reputation of West Bay, or Deadman's Bay, for its huge boundary of shingle, the Chesil Beach, which stretches from Portland towards Abbotsbury and Bridport, has proved to be the graveyard of many men and ships. In south-westerly gales, ships which could not round the Bill were driven into the bay and thrown upon the pebble bank, where they were quickly pounded to pieces. Over the centuries, many fine vessels met this terrible fate, and "wreckers" from Weymouth, Portland and Wyke Regis descended upon the beach to gather the harvest of cargo cast upon the shore.

With Portland Bill in sight, I eased the engine down, and slowly and carefully, we came in around the headland and continued our journey to Weymouth, arriving at about 3.30 p.m. No one questioned us, no Customs officer queried our arrival, so I tied up alongside Hope Quay. One of the local fishermen, "Darky" Warren, took me along the quay and introduced me to the mate in charge of the *Fusee II*. She was a tugboat-type vessel with a Polar diesel engine, built just before the First World War. Her main task was to transport fresh water to the forts, for which purpose she was equipped with two two-ton freshwater tanks; and she also conveyed stores, ammunition and personnel and did some target towing. She carried a crew of five, skippered by Tom Young, and had full sleeping facilities aboard. Her mate showed me to the Red Barracks on The Nothe. There I met Major David Lee, the Transport Officer, who already had an urgent job for me. I was to embark men from the Red Barracks and Nothe Fort, with their rifles and all their equipment, and take them out to the Breakwater Forts at Portland Harbour, a distance of just over two miles. The forts were manned by the Dorset Heavy Brigade, Royal Artillery, under Colonel Geoffrey Symes, and the Poole Regiment was also stationed at theforts from time to time under Major G. Yeatman.

Thus began my long acquaintanceship with Portland Harbour, a man-made harbour enclosing four square miles of safe anchorage, and over the years I was to become familiar with all its moods and caprices at every turn of wind and tide. The breakwaters had been built in the nineteenth century by convicts from Portland Prison, and the millions of tons of stone used in their construction were obtained from the quarries on Portland Island. Long before that, Sir Christopher Wren had selected the finest Portland limestone for the construction of St Paul's Cathedral, which was soon to become the symbol of resilience and hope for the people of war-torn London.

After disembarking the soldiers, we continued on to the other forts, picking up the men due to come ashore and landing them at Bincleaves. At the end of our first day, no accommodation was forthcoming, so Bert and I consumed what little food we had left and settled down for another night on the bare boards. I lay awake, turning over the events of the past two days in my mind. Knowing that Father was illiterate (as one of a large family which had fallen on hard times, he evaded school and crewed as ship's boy on the Plymouth sailing trawlers), I wondered just what he had signed in turning over the boat to the RASC, and what exactly was the standing of Bert and myself in all the confusion.

As the days passed, no food or accommodation was afforded us, and I had to buy oil and fuel for the boat from my own savings.

Work on the forts and defences and living quarters for the troops continued at a furious pace, although there was still no declaration of war. Barges carried building materials to the forts for gun emplacements, and beside our duty trips we were carrying out men of the Pioneer Corps to do this work. *My Girl* was detailed to take a huge load of straw to the forts for the soldiers' paliasses, and on that trip she resembled nothing so much as a floating haystack. Immediately after that trip, the boat was ordered to embark Colonel Geoffrey Symes and Regimental Sergeant Major Henry Crickmore (always known as Dick Crickmore) of the Royal Artillery, Red Barracks, and take them to the Breakwater Fort to oversee a night shooting exercise which would start about midnight. I was ordered to stand by for their return. I was already acquainted with Dick Crickmore from the days when the Dorset Heavy Brigade visited Fort Bovisand. He was an excellent drill instructor and I frequently heard his voice booming across Weymouth Harbour as he drilled the new recruits at the Red Barracks.

As soon as we reached the Breakwater Fort for the night shooting exercise, all the windows in the fort were opened prior to the guns firing, and the searchlights were in operation. Targets were towed across the bay by two fast launches, *Marlborough* and *Wellington*, and special winches on their sterns could be accelerated to pull the targets in at great bursts of speed when required. When the six-inch guns on the forts opened up, it was as if all hell had been let loose. The noise was deafening, and practically every sheet of glass in the windows was shattered.

In the early hours, I got the Colonel and the Sergeant Major aboard ready to return to Bincleaves. The wind had now strengthened considerably and the sea was coming in over the foredeck. Bert was at the pumps but the bilges were filling because they were choked with pieces of straw. I nursed the boat carefully back to Bincleaves, and by that time the water was lifting the floorboards. Once the two officers were ashore, Bert and I had to clear out the bilges, dismantle the pumps, and clean and re-assemble them ready for the first trip the next day. There was little sleep that night.

On the Sunday that war was declared, 3 September 1939, we were placed on full alert. I suddenly realised how vulnerable *My Girl* would be in air attacks; and Portland, as an important naval base, was bound to be a prime target for the enemy.

A full complement and cargo for us consisted of up to a hundred men and their equipment, ammunition and food rations. There were regular consignments of 50 shells each weighing half a hundredweight for the guns of the forts, together with 500 gallons of paraffin in five-gallon cans for the searchlight generators, plus my own boat fuel. An Instruction Book issued to us, on what to do if a fire broke out, stated in Paragraph 29, Section III:

"The first essential is the summoning of assistance. Immediately a fire breaks out, or is discovered, the alarm must be raised by shouting 'FIRE'. All personnel must be trained to shout 'FIRE' and keep on shouting until help arrives ..."

Although this seemed quite hilarious under the circumstances, such a situation did not bear too much thinking about. To make matters worse, *My Girl* as a former passenger launch was still painted overall in brilliant white, making her highly conspicuous by day and by night.

We continued on daily duties without any attack by the enemy. While we were on the Bincleaves turn of duty, we were on call for 24 hours each day. The alternative duty operated from Hope Quay and was meant to be on a weekly rota, but if we were inside Bincleaves when the boom defence was closed, we just had to stay there, and this took place quite frequently.

During my first visit to Weymouth and Portland in 1937, I had taken in little of my surroundings, for I was in a great hurry to be gone. Now the situation was different, and I had time to explore the area. When my first off-duty period came around, I decided to walk to Portland as it was a pleasant, sunny day. Visibility was such that the coastline down to Berry Head and Start Point was clear, and I looked longingly towards the west and home. Picking my way over the rocks and stone outcrops on the western side of the island, I glanced up to the top of the high cliffs.

As a boy, I had enjoyed cliff climbing at Bovisand, and I often ascended and descended the forbidding face of the Citadel Wall on Plymouth's Barbican without thinking of the dangerous drop below if I should fall. Perhaps my skill was in part a legacy from my forefathers who had to climb into the rigging of sailing ships and the men-o'-war deployed in the earlier days of the Royal Navy. My old love of climbing reasserted itself and I took on the challenge of those heights some 300 feet above me. There was quite a lot of scree, mostly the waste material from the quarries, and in places it was difficult to get a foothold. Partway up the cliff, a pinnacle of rock jutted forth, leaving a gap too wide to negotiate, so with some difficulty, I had to work my way around it.

At last, I reached the top, from where the view was quite spectacular. The vast sweep of West Bay was a fantastic blue in a flat calm, while a thin line of white surf marked its meeting with Chesil Beach.

To the other side of Chesil Beach lay the waters of the Fleet, then the narrow spit of land at Ferrybridge, and the great expanse of Portland Harbour. To the north and west, the sea was embraced by rolling green hills, the skyline above the village of Portesham dominated by the monument to its famous son, Thomas Masterman Hardy, who had sailed into battle with Nelson at Trafalgar. All about me was peaceful as I sat down to share the wonderful panorama with the seabirds wheeling on the warm currents of air. The war seemed nothing more than a bad dream. I was just about to get to my feet when there was a cry of "Halt!' and I was confronted with a soldier bearing an ominous-looking rifle. Fortunately, I was able to identify myself as being from the War Department by showing my pass, and after telephoning the Department for verification, the soldier directed me to a safe path, for I had unwittingly entered a minefield. Somewhat shaken by my experience, I set off to walk back to Weymouth; it was time to get back to duties aboard *My Girl*.

In mid-September, Britain was jolted into the harsh reality of war by the loss of the aircraft carrier HMS *Courageous* just two weeks after her departure from Portland. She encountered a U-boat off the Irish coast and sank with the loss of over 500 men only 15 minutes after two torpedoes struck her amidships. Further grim news came in October, when the Devonport-based battleship *Royal Oak* was torpedoed by a German submarine that had slipped into Scapa Flow and went down, taking over 800 men with her.

The lives of some of the lads I had grown up with in Plymouth were suddenly extinguished, and many homes mourned men who had been swallowed up by the sea.

The nights were growing considerably colder, but Bert and I still had no place to sleep other than the open boat under a sheet of canvas. It was difficult to get any meals, since the local cafes were closed by the time we came off-duty. Our situation was growing desperate; we had received no money other than a small sum to cover the journey from Plymouth to Weymouth, and I had to purchase all the oil and fuel for the boat myself. Other men whose boats had similarly been requisitioned were also without pay, although most of their vessels had sleeping quarters aboard. Bert and I were then supposed to sleep in the aftercabin aboard *Fusee II* but this was not a satisfactory arrangement, so it was finally suggested that we sleep in the Red Barracks, along with lorry drivers whose vehicles had been requisitioned, so we all bedded down on the Guard Room floor on palliasses.

Meals continued to be a problem, however, as our duties were subject to weather conditions and loading and unloading times. Barrack routine meant that all meals were finished by the time we returned from duty. At the end of our first nine weeks in Weymouth, we still had no wages, and only by drawing from my Post Office savings were we able to exist.

As withdrawals were limited to £3 per week, obtaining other lodgings was out of the question. Something had to be done to resolve our situation.

Here and there, crew members of other requisitioned or chartered vessels in the same plight as ourselves were beginning to desert and return home. Several steamboats formerly used as coal carriers around the coast of South Wales had been requisitioned to carry sand, cement and building blocks from Weymouth to the breakwaters for the building of the gun emplacements, and the stokers aboard them began to grow quite mutinous. One such vessel was the *Snowflake*, a double-ended Steam Puffer with a narrow "Woodbine" funnel, whose skipper, Captain Inskip, hailed from Plymouth. He was over 70 years of age at that time, and walked with a stick. A former P & O liner captain, he was a man of fine character.

After nearly nine weeks without pay, the stokers aboard *Snowflake* had had enough. Stoking the boilers was hot and thirsty work, and they did not have enough money to go to the pub for a drink at the end of the day, so they resolved to take matters into their own hands.

Two stokers, armed with a long slice bar from the furnace, glowing red hot, headed for the Transport Office and demanded to see the Officer in Charge. The clerks in the office got wind of what was coming and alerted Lieutenant

Scott, in his room directly above them. Lieutenant Scott called me up to the office while he telephoned for the police.

By now, the stokers were in the room below, but were unable to negotiate the narrow stairs to the officer's room with the 12 feet long bar, and the police soon arrived and warned them back on board their vessel.

I was later called before the Naval Officer based in the College buildings along the Dorchester Road and he informed me that all men whose vessels had been requisitioned would receive their pay in a short space of time. He advised me not to do as others had done, for if any man abandoned his boat and went home, he would send armed guards to bring him back again. I made it clear to him that I had never had any intention of deserting and this he accepted. He had been empowered to loan me some money until my pay came through, but I told him I would hold on a little longer, using my savings, as I did not want to go into his debt. It was a great relief to all when our pay eventually arrived.

Although we now had money in our pockets, Bert and I were unable to get leave to travel home to see our sister Doris get married in St Andrew's church, Plymouth. We had always been close as children, so it saddened us very much that we could not be present when she wed her sailor sweetheart before his ship sailed away into action.

As winter set in, the weather was atrocious at times, and gale force winds could make entry into Portland Harbour impossible. Weymouth Bay faces east, and consequently takes a pounding from gales from that quarter. On one occasion when the forts were calling for a boat, we started out from Weymouth to get to Portland Breakwater Fort. Only the East Ship Channel was open, and once we were outside Weymouth Harbour, huge breakers came sweeping over us and Bert had to pump out continuously. I eased down, trying to keep *My Girl* head on to the seas, for if we had come broadside, there was a great danger of capsizing. We had to go nearly over to White Nothe before shaping up for the East Ship Channel with the seas on the port quarter. Because of the heavy seas running, it was only when we eventually got in around the Breakwater Fort that the Naval PO signalman had been able to identify our boat.

All ships had to be identified by the Flag Officer in Charge, as an examination service and contraband control had been established. The six-inch guns of the Breakwater Fort were trained on incoming vessels until they hoisted the correct signal, and similar guns at the Nothe Fort were also at the ready. The examination anchorage in Weymouth Bay, which confiscated any cargo destined to help the enemy, seized over 140,000 tons of goods by the end of February 1940. An Irish vessel tried to run the gauntlet with a cargo of butter and other foodstuffs bound for Germany. She was berthed on the outside of other ships, and one morning she weighed anchor and tried to slip away, but a few shells across her bows from the Nothe Fort quickly brought her back.

As yet, there had been no bombing raids, but mines were a great hazard. One day we were approaching "A" Pierhead lighthouse and were about 200 yards off the breakwater, when we were hailed by a Navy motor launch. Its skipper shouted frantically through a megaphone: "Stop! Don't you see that mine there?" A mine was bobbing about in the water near the breakwater between the lighthouse and the Torpedo Depot, so it had to be disposed of as quickly as possible.

The Breakwater Lighthouse and East Ship Channel to Portland Harbour. *My Girl* experienced a close encounter with a drifting mine near this Breakwater.
(Courtesy HMS Osprey Photographic Unit)

There was much mine laying in the Channel in late 1939, particularly in the Shambles area off Portland. The Belgian ship *Alex van Opstal* was the first victim, to be followed by the Dutch merchantman *Binnendijk*, the Greek ship *Elena R* and later on the patrol vessel HMS *Kittiwake*. In 1940, the Germans began laying new types of mines, the magnetic mine and the acoustic mine. Magnetic mines were counteracted by the fitting of degaussing cables to the ships. By passing an electric current through these coils, a ship's magnetic field was reversed and the mine deactivated. Acoustic mines were destroyed by using sound waves to detonate them.

During the months of May and June 1940, many thousands of refugees passed through Weymouth as the Germans advanced relentlessly through Europe. Pleasure boats from Poole and Weymouth assisted with the evacuation of British and Allied troops from Dunkirk. Late in June, over 25,000 refugees from the Channel Islands came ashore at Weymouth. With German troops and planes poised for action just across the Channel, the war was about to enter a new and deadly phase, for the possibilities of invasion and air attacks were now very real.

Meanwhile, an older enemy of the soldier, sickness, suddenly stalked the Breakwater Forts. There was an outbreak of meningitis, and isolation was necessary to prevent the spread of that dreadful illness. *My Girl* was the only boat allowed to attend on the forts, bringing specialists and doctors to aid the victims. All the rations, medical supplies and mail had to be left on the camber jetty to be collected by the men on-duty. I remember that one desperately ill man was being brought ashore to hospital in Weymouth by a fast launch and his stretcher was laid on deck in the stern of the launch. Tragically the stretcher and the patient were washed overboard, with fatal consequences.

I believe several hundred men were affected by the disease, but of course, in wartime, information about such matters was restricted.

On 9 June 1940, HMS *Foylebank*, originally a merchantman and now converted to an anti-aircraft ship, arrived at Portland and anchored on "A" (Admiral's) buoy. She was preceded by a trawler sweeping a safe path for her, and one mine was exploded on her way into Portland Harbour – an omen, perhaps, of what was to follow before long.

Early on 20 June, several German planes circled Weymouth, releasing their cargo of bombs into the sea. Ten days later, on Sunday 30 June, I was off-duty and decided to walk to Portland. It was a beautiful summer day, and by late afternoon, I was approaching Yeates Corner at Portland, where people were strolling in the warm sunshine. In the distance, I heard the low hum of aircraft or seacraft, I couldn't be sure which. Then at a great height, I spotted three aircraft, and thinking they were our own planes, I was not unduly worried. Suddenly, however, bombs were whistling down, hitting the Verne and Chesil Beach.

The peaceful atmosphere of the afternoon was shattered as people scattered like leaves before the wind. These were the first bombs of the war for me, but *My Girl* and I were soon to be involved in many more bombings which took a toll of ships and lives. With the fall of the Channel Islands, the war had now arrived on our very doorstep.

June 1944. As D-Day approaches, American troops converge on
Weymouth prior to embarkation for Normandy. Here, troops are
shown marching down the Esplanade towards the Quay.
(Courtesy Weymouth Museum)

Dark Days

July 1940 brought the German war machine breathing down the backs of our necks. Fast motor torpedo boats were based on the French coast, and for the Luftwaffe stationed on the Cherbourg Peninsula, the flying time to the promontory of Portland was a mere 15 minutes or so. Sea and air strikes could come quickly, and we knew they would come soon.

On Thursday 4 July, I was on the Hope Quay turn of duty at Weymouth, starting with a trip to the forts at ten o'clock. Bert and I now had lodgings at Nothe cottages close to Nothe Fort, which afforded a view across Portland Harbour, and we were preparing to leave for duty at 8 a.m. when the air raid sirens sounded. Our landlady called us to the window and there we witnessed the terrible bombing of HMS *Foylebank*.

The attack on the *Foylebank* by the screaming dive-bombing Stukas was a savage one. Although it lasted only about eight minutes, she was hit by machine-gun fire and 22 bombs. Most of her guns were rendered useless when the electrical system was destroyed, but a young leading seaman, 23-year-old Jack Mantle, continued to fire the starboard pom-pom, although he was mortally wounded. He was awarded the Victoria Cross posthumously for his bravery, and Leading Seaman Cousins and Leading Seaman Gould each received the Distinguished Service Medal.

In subdued mood, we loaded personnel and details at Hope Quay and proceeded with *My Girl* to the Breakwater Forts. By now, *Foylebank* was burning and slowly sinking, presenting a sad and desolate sight. A huge pall of black smoke drifted across the harbour. Other ships in Portland Harbour at the time also suffered damage in the raid, and the attack suddenly brought home the vulnerability of the harbour, whose defences were found to be weak. The Shambles Lightship was a potential navigation aid to the enemy, so its crew were taken off and the light extinguished. She was later towed into Portland Harbour, where she remained for the duration of the war.

Throughout July and August, and into September, fierce bombing raids continued over Weymouth and Portland, some carried out by lone raiders, but many others involving larger formations of aircraft. All those working in the defence of the two harbours were to experience long hours of duty, characterised by tension and tiredness, but the civilian population was also subject to the state of constant alertness that prevailed in the area. Shipping losses in the Channel off the Dorset coast were enormous as vessels were regularly dive-bombed, harassed by E-boats, or fell victim to mines. Spitfires from nearby Warmwell Aerodrome and their pilots participated in savage engagements with enemy planes over Portland and were in the thick of the Dorset coast sector of the Battle of Britain.

The threat of invasion hung in the air like a heavy thundercloud, and while the country watched and waited, the Channel coastline braced itself against the expected arrival of German forces to storm our shores.

A massive raid was carried out on Portland Harbour installations by over 150 German planes on Sunday 11 August 1940. *My Girl* was lying in Bincleaves beside an iron barge. Bert and I had taken out the floorboards and stacked them on the open barge while we cleaned out the bilges. The air raid sirens sounded, and Bert went for shelter. I remained on the boat, beneath the canvas canopy folded across the frame above my head. Bombs began to rain down around me and I threw myself into the bottom of my boat as the shipwright's store nearby on shore received a direct hit. Debris hurtled skywards in a terrific explosion and pieces of shrapnel flew past me, embedding themselves in the timbers of *My Girl*.

As the dust began to clear, I climbed out of the boat, and keeping behind the electricians' hut for shelter, I looked along the Breakwater. The German planes swooped low over the surface of the sea and I heard the rattle of machine-gun fire. I saw to my horror that their target was the young errand boy from Avant's, the Weymouth butchers, who had just made a delivery to HMS *Vernon*, the torpedo depot on the Breakwater. As he ran back along the causeway, crying in terror while bullets danced around him like hailstones, I shouted and gestured to him, "Get down! Get down between the rocks!"

For a few agonising seconds, he seemed paralysed by fear before scrambling down between the great boulders of the Breakwater. More bombs whistled down, some just missing the Breakwater and plunging into the sea, sending great columns of water rising into the air. Eventually, I got to the boy and dragged him, still crying and shaking, into a nearby sandbagged gun emplacement. The raid continued in its ferocity.

"God, this is it!" I thought. "This is the invasion." But I was determined that I wasn't going to stand around and wait to be killed. The anti-aircraft gun within our shelter had its ammunition belt in place, so I told the boy to feed it through, and although I had been given no gunnery training, I aimed the gun at the planes as they veered out to sea and fired away.

Beside the direct hit to the store at Bincleaves, some 90 bombs fell on Weymouth and Portland, causing considerable damage in the area. The railway line was also hit and two oil tanks were damaged, the escaping oil burning fiercely for some time. When the "All clear" sounded at last, a message came from the Nothe Fort to the policeman on-duty at Bincleaves, asking who had fired the gun, and I was named. However, I received no reprimand, and a directive was issued later that all War Department boat crew should undertake gunnery training. I duly attended a course, from which I passed out as being qualified in the firing, cleaning and oiling of various guns, including Lewis, Hotchkiss, Marlin, Browning, Colt, Oerlikon and rocket guns.

Our gunnery training courses took place in the Southampton and New Forest areas. A motor coach took us into part of the forest one day for shotgun practice with clay pigeon targets, and we then went on to gain experience with rocket guns which were housed inside steel turrets.

The interior of one building used for simulation night firing exercises had a high, domed ceiling which represented a darkened sky. As soon as I was seated at the gun and strapped into the harness, the instructor informed me that a plane, for example a Junkers Ju 88, was approaching from a certain quarter. Then, complete with appropriate sound effects, a bright dot, similar to a plane caught in a searchlight beam, began to move across the ceiling, and when I fired the gun, another light flashed up to pinpoint my aim on the target.

I passed all these tests with flying colours, but my experience with the Oerlikon gun gave my instructor quite a shock. The Oerlikon was set up inside a large room at the Board of Trade offices in Southampton, and as I strapped myself into the seat aboard the gun, its eight feet long barrel was pointing down at the floor. The body weight of the operator had to act as a counterbalance with this particular gun, but I was of very light build, so that when the instructor ordered me to cock the gun, it wouldn't move.

In desperation after several abortive attempts to raise the barrel, I jumped down upon the seat with all my strength, whereupon the barrel suddenly shot upwards and the muzzle of the gun brought down a six feet square chunk of the ceiling with a thunderous crash. My instructor was ashen-faced.

"That's enough!" he spluttered through the clouds of dust. "You've passed!"

August 1940 was to witness many fierce engagements over Dorset as our planes battled with the enemy, and during the second half of that month, German bombers returned to the Weymouth and Portland areas almost every day. Another heavy raid took place in September, causing damage to installations in the naval base. The threat of invasion remained high, and I received written instructions detailing me, in the event of an enemy landing, to take off the cylinder heads from the engine of my vessel and throw them overboard.

We had some very close calls during air raids when *My Girl* was ploughing between the forts and the mainland carrying men and ammunition, shells and paraffin. Looking back now, it seems truly miraculous that we came safely through those terrifying experiences.

An alarming incident happened one day when we were landing men and stores at the Breakwater Forts in heavy seas, though it had nothing to do with the enemy. Bert kept the boat in as close as possible to the wall of the breakwater, hanging on to the rungs of an iron ladder with a heavy boathook.

A great wave jolted the boat with the result that the boathook catapulted backwards, striking the mast of *My Girl* with tremendous force. The power of the impact was such that the stout timber of the mast snapped in half with an ear-splitting crack. Luckily that was our only casualty. We had to replace the mast quickly for we used it to carry recognition lights. Their sequence was regularly changed, and when challenged at night, all boats had to display the correct signal lights immediately.

The Weymouth lifeboat *William and Clara Ryland*, which was on continuous alert as our planes engaged with the enemy, was frequently called out to search for pilots who had ditched into the sea. I got to know "Mac" – Mr MacDermott, the chief engineer – who incidentally fashioned the new mast for *My Girl*. When I was not on-duty, I crewed on the lifeboat if they were short-handed.

One afternoon, we went out to search for two Spitfire pilots who had come down off Portland Bill. We had no success. A message then came through on the radio receiver to search for a pilot in West Bay, off Bridport, but the coastguard got in touch with us later to say that the Yacht Patrol was already out, so we returned to Weymouth Harbour. I earned a reprimand from my Major the next day, who said that although I had been off-duty, my priority was to remain on service call. It was a tough time for the lifeboatmen, as they often got machine-gunned by the enemy whilst picking up survivors at sea.

When the war was over, I was to resume my link with the lifeboat service, assisting with the delivery of lifeboats to refitting stations as well as with rescue work.

On 17 November 1940, Weymouth experienced its worst explosion of the war. Bert and I had lodgings in Newberry Terrace in the Chapelhay area at the time. We were awaiting the 9 p.m. news on the wireless, as it was expected that Winston Churchill would speak, when there was an almighty explosion and the front window of the house was blown in. Glass showered everywhere, the electricity was cut off, and everything was plunged into darkness. A German raider had cut his engine and then dropped a parachute mine which was probably intended for Weymouth Harbour. The havoc was terrible. Some 77 houses were destroyed and 879 were damaged. Trinity School had been hit, and the whole Chapelhay area was a shambles. Many lives were lost on that dreadful night.

1941 brought concentrated bombing raids on towns and cities by German planes. Blitz! A new and terrible word entered our language as the blitzkrieg began. In March, Plymouth was pounded and incendiaries set the whole city on fire. Bombed and burned, the old city I knew so well passed away, and with it went our home and all our possessions. Bert and I were desperate for news of our family, and we were greatly relieved to hear that our parents were safe, having taken shelter in the Citadel dungeons. In certain shelters, all those inside had suffocated in the great heat generated by the fires raging all around, and these were simply sealed up with their dead inside. We were thankful when confirmation came that our sister Doris was safe and well.

Mother and Father were homeless, for our lovely new flat at Hoegate Street, together with its furnishings, was blasted off the face of the earth. But they were alive, when thousands had died. The only item mother had taken to the shelter with her was a small attaché case containing personal papers, documents and a little money, together with Father's medals. Father was very proud of his medals from the 1914-18 war, including one presented to him by Tsar Nicholas II while his ship HMS *Jupiter* was involved in convoy duties to Russia.

Finding somewhere to live was a desperate problem for my parents, for practically every house around them had been demolished and Plymouth now had an army of homeless people. It was bitterly cold, and I managed to buy some blankets at Dennisons shop, near the Echo office in Weymouth, and mailed them to my mother.

Bombing raids on Portland Harbour continued. On 5 June 1941, there was a particularly heavy raid. Early that morning, I had spent some time talking to Gunner George Younger when he came off-duty. He was 61, one of the oldest servicemen I ferried to and from the forts.

He told me that he was going to take his wife and daughter to stay with relatives in Bournemouth, because the bombing had become so bad at Chapelhay.

At 9 p.m., *My Girl* was at Bincleaves preparing for the trip to the forts. About a dozen soldiers were already in the boat and others were going along the Breakwater to embark. A thick haze hung over Portland Harbour, masking the sudden approach of a Junkers Ju 88. It swooped low over the coal hulk *Himalaya* and with cannon blazing from the nose of the plane, it riddled the stern of the boat, killing the night watchman, "Science" Jacketts. The *Himalaya*, badly holed, sank in a matter of minutes.

Shells were pounding the Breakwater, but *My Girl* lay inside the Torpedo Works jetty, and was thus afforded some shelter. The soldiers were re-embarking when someone shouted that George Younger had been hit and was lying in the road. I ran to where he lay in a pool of blood. He was terribly wounded. A doctor was summoned from the main gate and an ambulance requested from Portwey Hospital. I helped lift George on to the stretcher and into the ambulance. *My Girl* continued on the duty trip, returning to Bincleaves at 11 p.m., and landed details. I moored up and ceased duty at midnight.

The next day, I learned that George was dead. Shrapnel had torn through his shoulder, travelled right through his body, and finally embedded itself in his hand. The doctor spoke to me and showed me the piece of shrapnel. It was the base or "heel" of a shell, and the secret which he and I shared was the fact that the shell was British. The markings on it were proof. The old warrior had been killed in the crossfire.

An entry in the log of *My Girl* dated 16 August 1941 states that Bert and I "accepted the conditions of the War Department Fleet". Having also passed the medical examinations, we now had official standing with the War Department. Although I did not know it at the time, Father had received Notice of Acquisition of *My Girl*. With no address to reply from, Father engaged Tamlyn's Shipping Agents on the Parade at Plymouth to negotiate terms for the sale of the boat to the War Department.

Meanwhile, Bert and I were again without lodgings. Fortunately a house in Nothe Parade had been taken over by 615 Water Transport Company for offices, and we were allocated a bedroom. The house had been empty and allowed to run down for a considerable time, and needed a lot of cleaning up. Mr MacDermott – Lifeboat "Mac" - loaned me a vacuum cleaner and I went over the house from top to bottom, emptying the cleaner eight or nine times in the process. With two iron beds, and a table and two chairs issued by the Red Barracks, we settled in. Although there was no heating and the roof leaked, it was better than sleeping in the open boat or on the guardroom floor. One blessing was that Mrs Mac supplied us with three meals a day, which were greatly appreciated.

From 12 July to 18 August 1941, *My Girl* underwent a complete overhaul at the shipyard belonging to Cosens & Co. of Weymouth. Between voyages to the forts with another vessel, the *Estrelita*, Bert and I worked on *My Girl*, scraping, varnishing and anti-fouling, while Cosens's men serviced the engine and built a cabin to afford some protection. As soon as *My Girl* had been officially acquired by the War Department, her white paintwork had by order to be covered by grey, and while it saddened us to have to do this, her new colour at least rendered her less of a target to the enemy. The boat was no longer ours, but Father was promised the first chance to buy her back at the end of the war.

Several officers at the forts told me they would bid for her when the war was over, but I was determined that she would eventually return to us and re-emerge from her drab colours into the swan that she truly was.

Estrelita, a requisitioned motor yacht, was an awkward vessel to handle, although she was sturdily built. She was some 36 feet in length with only a nine foot beam, and she had a canoe stern. Her forecabin gave some shelter from the elements. One day, when strong easterly winds pounded Weymouth Bay, I warned the officer and men aboard that we had a rough passage ahead, but on looking across the comparative calm of the harbour, the officer was scornful of my advice.

The men settled down below deck, anticipating a bumpy ride, while the officer seated himself on a canvas folding stool in the centre of the cabin. Rounding the Stone Pier, we met the first big swell and the bows of the *Estrelita* took a nose dive and then reared up again. The officer shot up off his stool, hitting his head on the deck beam above. He then fell back on to the stool which promptly folded up beneath him, to the ill-concealed amusement of the assembled company. Much mortified, the officer continued the journey with greater regard for his safety.

During stormy crossings, it sometimes proved difficult for officers to maintain a dignified stance. Paradoxically I had to give the orders when disembarking in heavy seas, and as the boat rose and fell beside the landing area, I would shout to officers and men alike: "Jump when I tell you ... now!"

Another unfortunate incident involved the aforementioned officer during disembarkation at Bincleaves when the weather was very bad and the boom defences were closed. I had to get alongside the Torpedo Depot Pier and the men had to climb an iron ladder alongside the wall. As he ascended the ladder, the officer's baton slipped and fell into deep water. Much to his dismay, it was irretrievable. Some of us knew the baton concealed a stiletto blade, a reminder that in the grimness of war, self-defence could mean survival.

Rough weather often meant that another vessel engaged in carrying men to and from the forts declined to sail. I would have preferred not to sail in very bad seas, but I knew that vital supplies had to be got through. The soldiers longed for relief from their cramped conditions at the forts, and when precious leave was granted, many had to get to Weymouth Station to catch an early train home. They knew I would come, whatever the weather, and that I would get them ashore safely. I put my trust in my long experience of such conditions, and I knew that, at least in *My Girl*, I had a sound boat beneath me. That the seas around Weymouth and Portland can be a testing place in storms was to be demonstrated again in October 1948, after the end of the war, when a liberty boat taking men from Weymouth to the aircraft carrier HMS *Illustrious* in Portland Harbour foundered, with the loss of 29 lives.

On 12 September 1941, Bert was involved in an accident on the boat, but we did not realise the significance of his injury when it occurred. We were at Hope Quay loading stores for the forts. Because the tide was very low, there was a drop of about 12 feet from the quayside to the bottom of the boat. I stood on the seat of the boat to receive the crates being passed down, and stowed them on deck to ensure an even load. Bert was assisting with stowing when he suddenly let out a yell of pain. A crate had been dropped from the quayside and had struck him on the knee.

Pale and shaken though he was, he insisted that he could continue with the duty, and *My Girl* duly delivered the stores to the forts. Later that day, I entered an accident report in my ship's log.

For the next few days, Bert limped around in great discomfort. I reported to the army officer at the Transport Office and asked that Bert be allowed to see the doctor. The officer advised that Bert should rest his leg for three or four days, and that there was nothing to worry about. A temporary hand would undertake his work and he would continue to receive his pay. The knee grew steadily worse, and I had to bring Bert's meals from Mrs Mac, as he was unable to walk even that short distance. Again I approached the army officer and requested that Bert be seen by the doctor. He was not seen, but instead a medical orderly travelling in the boat the next day gave me a box of ointment which had been prescribed by the doctor for Bert to rub into his knee.

In the days that followed, I grew increasingly anxious about leaving my brother alone all day, but I had to continue my duties on war service. One evening, I came off-duty at 6 p.m. and hurried upstairs to see him. I was shocked to see how ill he looked, and I knew I had to get him to a doctor as soon as possible. Struggling along in the blackout, I carried Bert on my back to Dr Robert Devereux's surgery at 22 Trinity Road. At last, our turn came to see the doctor. When I rolled up his trouser leg for his knee to be examined, it was obvious that the injury was even worse than I had feared. After a quick inspection, the doctor said grimly, "This man must be got into hospital as soon as possible."

In reply to his questioning, I told him that we were from Plymouth and he again said, "If this man is not got into hospital without delay, I wash my hands of his case!" I carried Bert back to his bedroom and tried to work out how to cope with the situation. I telephoned Plymouth for a message to be given to my parents, telling them that Bert would be on the Royal Blue coach the next day and he must be met and got into hospital with the utmost urgency. In the morning, I ordered a taxi and took my brother to the bus station and put him on the coach. It was with a heavy heart that I returned to duty. Bert was taken to the South Devon and East Cornwall Hospital in Plymouth and eventually, after a desperate battle against infection in the days before antibiotics were available, his leg had to be amputated. The news was a devastating blow to me and to my parents, and the tragedy of the situation tormented me for weeks afterwards, as Bert remained in hospital, ill and depressed. If only I had insisted on the army doctor seeing him! If only I had got him to Dr Devereux sooner!

As the months passed, Bert was sent to the Atlantic Hospital in Newquay to convalesce, and later still he went to Exeter Hospital for several minor operations and the fitting of an artificial limb.

He was then able to return to live with my parents in their temporary home, where Mother had to do the daily dressings and cope with his depression.

Two years of poor accommodation and the difficulties we had in obtaining our meals, such as they were under rationing, took their toll on both of us, but Bert's health was so seriously undermined after his accident that he was discharged from War Department service in December 1941.

There followed a succession of able seamen and ship's boys assigned to *My Girl* after Bert's departure. Billy Brown was a young man who later emigrated to New Zealand when the "block ship" (a vessel used to bar the entrance to Weymouth Harbour at night during the war) sailed there on her first post-war voyage. Another mate was Albert Holland, who was one of a large family of brothers in Weymouth connected with fishing, boating and the lifeboat service. Others included Nelson Smith, who became a bus conductor after the war, and Cyril Johnson and Bob Arnold. Bill Northey, who hailed from my native Plymouth, joined me aboard *My Girl* for a brief spell later in the war, and he was followed by Bert Brown. Each War Department vessel carried a ship's boy. Among ours were Bob Smallbone and Freddie Roberts. Freddie was a little Cockney lad who always arrived for duties at the very last minute as the boat was leaving the quay, running like the wind or pedalling furiously on a borrowed bicycle.

On return visits to Plymouth during brief spells of leave, I felt like a stranger in my own city, such was the extent of the destruction there. The ruins of St Andrew's church, the nave wide open to the sky, represented the only landmark I recognised. My home, my street, my old school, and the very heart of the city, had disappeared into a sea of rubble. A whole new temporary shopping area had to be established at Mutley Plain, away from the grim conditions of the old city centre. And still the bombing continued. A huge sugar store was hit and in the heat of the ensuing fire, all the sugar inside melted and flowed out in a boiling river across the quay and into the harbour. Also being dropped were delayed action bombs, which exploded as people returned to the ruins of their homes to search for relatives, or to retrieve bits and pieces of their belongings, adding to the horror and misery of the situation.

As 1941, with its many dark days, drew to a close, it was marked as the year of the passing of some of Britain's greatest ships. In May, the mighty battle cruiser HMS *Hood* and the heavy cruiser *York* had gone down. November and December brought news of the sinking of the aircraft carrier *Ark Royal* and the battleships *Repulse*, *Prince of Wales*, *Queen Elizabeth* and *Valiant*. In addition to the losses incurred by the Royal Navy, the merchant fleet had suffered greatly.

Within my small bedroom above the Transport Office at Weymouth, I felt more lonely and dispirited than I had ever felt before in my life, or have ever felt since. In the space of a few months, my home, my boat and my brother had all been wrenched from me. The final shock came when my mother contacted me with the news that she had been sent a bill for several hundred pounds for Bert's hospital treatment. She was distraught over the matter, since there was no way that she could find such a sum of money. I contacted a local solicitor for advice, but weeks went by and nothing seemed to be happening. Finally, in desperation, I decided I would write to Nancy, Lady Astor, who was well known among the fishermen of her waterfront constituency at Plymouth for her championship of the rights of women and children. In the poorest days of my boyhood, when Mother sent me to the soup kitchen on Green Street for the jug of soup and half a loaf of bread which had to provide a day's meal for our family of five, it was Lady Astor who often ladled out the lentil soup for me and the people in the queue.

I sent off my letter to Lady Astor and waited anxiously for the post each day to bring her reply. Surely there had to be some way to resolve our dreadful situation.

Bert Hill, Mrs. "Mac" and Ron Hill, Summer 1941, just before
Bert's tragic accident. Bert loved the cinema – here, he is doing his
Buster Keaton "Stoneface" impression. (Author's Collection)

Bert Hill off-duty with James MacDermott and Mrs. "Mac",
Summer 1941. Just before the shutter clicked, Bert switched hats
with Mrs. "Mac". (Author's Collection)

The Turn of the Tide

The consequences of my brother's accident aboard the boat continued to haunt me through the lonely days following his departure from Weymouth. In war-torn Plymouth, my parents were being pressed for payment of Bert's hospital bills, and in melancholy mood, I watched and waited for the post each day, hoping that a reply to my appeal to Lady Astor might ease their plight. I tried to wait for the mail before leaving on the Hope Quay duty, in case the long-awaited letter arrived. By this time, more and more women were coming forward to take on the jobs vacated by the men away at war, and I suddenly realised that a postwoman, neatly dressed in a navy blue trouser suit, now delivered the mail in the Chapelhay area, including Nothe Cottages, Bincleaves and the Transport Office on the harbourside.

One morning, just before I boarded the boat, the postwoman came along the quay.

"Good morning," I ventured respectfully. 'Is there a letter for Mr Ron Hill of the Transport Office?"

"I'm sorry," she replied kindly. "The rules are that all mail must be delivered to the address on the envelope."

I was rather taken aback, but of course, she was right. She had no way of knowing who I was, or my reason for asking. I found myself explaining and telling her of the worry concerning my parents and my brother, and she listened sympathetically, agreeing with me about the suffering that the war had brought about.

When she told me that she had lost her mother and father in the early years of the war, I felt a little ashamed at having dwelt so deeply on my own troubles, for her loss was greater than my own. There was no letter for me that day, but as I jumped aboard the boat, I somehow felt relief in having had someone to talk to. Also, there was a feeling of a shared bond between us, although I did not even know her name.

The very next day, I received a beautifully written letter from Lady Astor saying, "If you do not hear from the War Department within seven days of this letter arriving, I will bring the matter up in the House." A few days later, my mother wrote to me, saying that she had been informed that all the expenses for Bert's operation and hospitalisation would be paid for by the War Department. The burden of that awful worry had at last been lifted from our shoulders.

I no longer had any urgent need to wait for the morning mail, yet I hoped to see the postwoman again and tell her my news. But the days passed and we did not meet. It seemed that she was on-duty in another area of the town. I realised that she had helped me to put my own troubles into perspective, but I began to wonder how she was coping with hers. Did she have any relatives to help her after the death of her parents? Where did she live, and what was her name? I longed to see her again.

With the problem of the hospital bill now resolved, I was experiencing a reaction which I could not define. The daily routine tasks seemed irksome, and as the war dragged on, it all seemed to be so futile. Whereas previously I had slept well through sheer tiredness, I was now lying awake through the night hours for no apparent reason.

A week later, I saw her again, coming along the quayside. As she was on-duty, we could only have a few words, although there was so much I wanted to ask her. She was obviously pleased when I told her that my special letter had arrived.

"You know my name – Ron Hill," I said. "I'd like to know yours."

She was sifting through the letters in her hand and reaching for the next letterbox. Then turning, she said, "My name is Dolores."

I caught my breath. What a beautiful and unusual name! "It's Spanish, and it means 'sorrowful'," she added.

I struggled to find the right things to say, remembering the sadness in her life, but no words came.

I looked up and her eyes were sparkling. Was she teasing me? Had she already guessed that I was falling in love with her?

"I live with my married sister and her children. Her husband's in the Navy, serving abroad." She volunteered that information without my having to ask for it, and I was thankful for that. People were passing by. I stepped back to avoid them and she was gone.

Weeks passed before we met again, and during that time of waiting, I was torn by alternating feelings of hope and despair. If I told her of my love, would it spell the end of our new-found friendship? Was there someone else? What if I had to put her out of my life forever? My room seemed cold and cheerless. Bert's iron bedstead was stripped to the bare mattress. I grieved as I thought of the long hours when he had suffered there without complaining. What could he make of life now? He certainly would never work on the boat again. What if the boat was never ours again? There was no guarantee that she would be, even if she survived the bombs and mines. All the struggles of my life, the long and painful climb to brief success, seemed to count for nothing. My books and my few boyhood treasures were now dust and ashes in the ruins of my home. Only sentimental ties remained.

The memories of sunlit beaches at Cawsand and Bovisand, the soft drone of voices on the summer air, the swish of the bow wave and the gentle lapping of waves against the boat, the laughter of children, the rhythm of guitars on evening trips homeward – the aching and yearning became intolerable.

The view from my window was bleak. The harbour was grey with mist and rain, and only wartime craft were tied alongside the quay. The beach beyond was barricaded and deserted, and at strategic points around the town, rows of "dragons' teeth" tank traps waited to ensnare enemy invaders. God, it was cold! I was thankful when the next spell of duty came around to break the misery, but I had at least come to one decision – I would tell Dolores of my love for her. I had nothing to offer her. My situation could be summed up in the phrase applied to the bombed out and homeless; I had only the clothes I stood up in, but all else had gone. True, I had been issued with a gold-braided uniform befitting the skipper of a vessel on His Majesty's service, but in truth, serge trousers, seaman's jersey, reefer coat and cap were more suited to my heavy duties, and today was certainly going to be one for seaboots and oilskins. "Get on with it, then," I told myself.

I brought *My Girl* into Bincleaves about 3 p.m. one afternoon and the soldiers disembarked. The post usually came to the Bincleaves office about that time, and if Dolores was on-duty, I might see her. However, she had already handed in the mail. I tied up the boat and made my way along the shore path to where I hoped she would still be making deliveries. The path led to a narrow passage aptly named "The Lookout", for this vantage point afforded a marvellous view across Portland Harbour, Weymouth Bay and the cliffs beyond. The sea was bright, and the spring sunshine gently warming.

She must have known that our meeting was not accidental. We talked for a while of unimportant things, but I was wrestling to put my feelings into words. There was an awkward silence, and she made as if to leave. I caught her in my arms and we embraced. There was no need for words; our love was sealed in that special moment.

"I must go now," she said.

"Of course."

She had the responsibility of His Majesty's mail and I had the responsibility of men's lives. We parted, knowing that we would meet again and again. As I returned to the boat, I felt that life for me now had new meaning and purpose. The tide had turned for me and the feelings of isolation and despair were ebbing away. Dolores was my first and only love: and she still is.

Dolores introduced me to her sister, Rubea. Both girls had Spanish names, Rubea meaning red because of her Titian hair. Their brother, although baptised in Spain, was given the traditional family name of William. As a young man, their father enlisted in the Royal Artillery. His first station was at Golden Hill Fort at Freshwater, Isle of Wight, near the family home at Elm Cottage. Later postings included Gosport and Queenstown; and finally he went to Gibraltar, where married quarters were provided for him, his wife and their little ones at Dagnino's Buildings. When I happened to mention that George Younger, who had been tragically killed at Bincleaves, had also been in the Royal Artillery, Dolores told me to my great surprise that George was buried next to her father.

The raids on Portland Harbour which I witnessed were terrible enough, but the enemy bombs were not reserved for the harbour installations alone. The civilian population of Weymouth and Portland suffered greatly as homes, shops and offices were reduced to rubble. Her job brought Dolores close to the physical and emotional devastation experienced by ordinary folk as the result of the war. Delivering mail in the Chapelhay area was particularly difficult, for that part of the town had been badly damaged. Here and there, some families were still trying to shelter in the ruins of their homes. Ironically, in many cases where houses were bombed, only the front doors were left standing in their frames where once little homes had been cherished, their letterboxes sighing in the wind. After each successive raid, bundles of mail had to be marked "bombed out" and initialled, then returned to the sorting office to be filed with "destroyed by enemy action" cards.

The women waiting at home watched anxiously for the arrival of the post, and envelopes with black edges brought the tidings that they dreaded most of all. Throughout one day's duty at Hope Quay, I heard the most agonising crying and wailing from one of the little houses huddled together along the quay: "Harry! My poor Harry!"

When I enquired further, I learned that the sorrowing woman in the house had received news that her only son, all she had in the world, had been killed in action.

Another sad story was that of a dear lady who waited at her gate daily for Dolores, hoping for news of her son who was a prisoner of war in Germany. She somehow always managed a smile, in spite of her disappointment as Dolores passed by. Then one morning, a prisoner of war letter card turned up at the sorting office, with its few cryptic sentences deleted as necessary – "I am well/I am not well", etc. Dolores felt happy that she could at last deliver this crumb of comfort. However, when she turned into Milton Road, there was no one waiting at the gate. Instead, a huge crater contained the rubble of the little bungalow where the lady had lived.

By late 1941, the focus of the war was gradually changing, with the threat of invasion diminishing as German troops were committed to the Russian front. However, raids on Channel convoys by planes and E-boats continued to take a heavy toll. The entry of America into the war after the bombing of Pearl

Harbour by the Japanese in December 1941 was an event of great significance. Early in 1942, the first American servicemen arrived in Britain and officers and signalmen were based on the middle arm of the Portland Breakwater, while gunners and smokescreen specialists were located at the "Hood" end of the old outer breakwater, which was about a mile and a half long. I was soon assisting with the ferrying of these men between the forts and the mainland, and always found them cheerful and friendly. The few orders that I had to give, mainly in bad weather, were met with a prompt, "Yes, Sir!"

On 2 April 1942, German dive-bombers made another attack upon Weymouth, killing 20 people and injuring 56. The *Dorset Daily Echo* offices received a direct hit, while the Post Office was in a direct line only about a hundred yards away.

Dolores and I had both experienced several near misses as bombs whistled earthwards, and I became more and more anxious about her, and increasingly concerned as to what the future held for us. We wanted to marry, but wondered if we should wait until this dark era was over. Accommodation was in short supply after the destruction of so many properties, and furnishing a home was almost an impossibility in the age of ration books and coupons. How long was this dreadful war going on, and would we survive it?

As I was pondering over the trials and tribulations I had endured in my life, including the times I had been saved from disaster at sea, everything suddenly seemed to me to be part of a plan which I could now understand. Fate had decreed that I found harbour in Weymouth after the Channel Islands adventure, an incident that led in turn to the determining of my posting to Weymouth on war service. If it had been otherwise, I would not have met the woman I wanted to marry. Just as we had resolved to wed that summer, our hopes were seemingly dashed by an order from the War Department: *My Girl* and I were to be sent to Sierra Leone, to undertake similar work there.

Fate was to intervene again, however, for at the eleventh hour as I was preparing to be sent abroad, and *My Girl* was ready to be taken to Liverpool for shipment, the order was rescinded. I learned later that the Officer in Charge at Weymouth had appealed against the decision by the War Department to send me abroad, because he considered that *My Girl* was "absolutely indispensable" at Weymouth.

During our courtship, although our time together was governed by the regulations of wartime and the long hours of duty, we loved to walk together. Dolores had a love of poetry and painting, and I gained a new appreciation of the world around me. My eyes, previously more accustomed to the wide vistas of seascapes, became better acquainted with the beauty of the countryside surrounding Weymouth. That springtide was special, despite the savage battles being fought about us in the seas and skies. Even though the houses were in ruins, the trees and flowers around them budded and blossomed and the birds still sang.

As we sat together in the lovely Nothe Gardens overlooking the sea, Dolores introduced me to the poetry of John Masefield, the sailor poet, whose verses of *Sea Fever* were a revelation to me. Now I could identify what it was that drew men back to the sea again and again, for the poet's words expressed my own feelings more perfectly than I could ever hope to do:

I must go down to the seas again, to the lonely sea and the sky,
And all I ask is a tall ship and a star to steer her by,
And the wheel's kick and the wind's song and the white sails
  shaking,
And a grey mist on the sea's face and a grey dawn breaking.

I must go down to the seas again, for the call of the running tide
Is a wild call and a clear call that may not be denied;
And all I ask is a windy day with the white clouds flying
And the flung spray and the blown spume, and the sea-gulls
  crying.

I must go down to the seas again, to the vagrant gypsy life,
To the gull's way and the whale's way where the wind's like a
  whetted knife;
And all I ask is a merry yarn from a laughing fellow-rover
And quiet sleep and a sweet dream when the long trick's over.

Dolores asked me what was meant by the "wheel's kick" and I explained how, in very rough seas when holding on to the steering wheel to keep the ship on course, a heavy wave would hit the rudder, giving the wheel a terrific jerk or "kick". I soon learned the verses and my rendering of the poem pleased her: she thought I had just the right voice for it.

We lingered over those lovely lines as we gazed out over the sea and longed for the time when we would be able to go sailing together.

We had a lucky escape when I was walking Dolores home to her sister's house one evening in the blackout. The air raid sirens sounded as we passed St Paul's church and drew level with Holly Road. We heard the first bomb come whistling down and threw ourselves behind a garden wall as it hit the houses in Holly Road with a terrific explosion, completely demolishing them. We clung together in the darkness, hoping there would not be a second bomb, for it surely would have killed us. There was a long silence, broken by the agonised wailing of a man as he regained consciousness amid the ruins of his home: "My house! My house! My house!" Despite the uncertainty ahead, one thing only was sure: Dolores and I loved each other and that would be our security in life, that would enable us to face the future together. When we were married on 8 August 1942 at St Paul's Church, Weymouth, there were no bells ringing for me and my girl. Church bells throughout the land were stilled during the war, and the breaking of their silence at that time would have proclaimed an enemy invasion. (They were rung in thanksgiving for the victory of El Alamein and again at Christmas 1942.)

My parents were able to travel from Plymouth for our wedding, but Bert was unwell and had to remain at home. Doris did not attend either, for the happier reason that she was awaiting the arrival of her first child in the autumn. Among the presents we have always treasured were some beautiful china from the American servicemen on the Breakwater Forts, and a bound volume of John Masefield's poems from an old sea friend of the family, Patrick Brophy.

We were able to snatch a few days for our honeymoon at Bournemouth and then travelled to Plymouth to spend a little time there. My parents now had rooms in a terraced house near the Hoe, and even while we were staying with them a bombing raid occurred, turning Coates's Plymouth Gin factory, less than a hundred yards away, into a raging inferno.

Just as the tide had turned in my own life, the tide of war was starting to turn in favour of the Allies. The last Allied defeat in Europe had occurred late in 1941, and by July 1942, the German army had been halted in North Africa and the British then took the offensive. The battle of El Alamein, early in November, was to prove to be the turning point of the war. In the meantime, however, Allied shipping continued to incur heavy losses through mines and the activities of U-boats, with the result that food and fuel shortages grew worse, but the tables were to be turned gradually with the development of radar and sonar devices and the use of destroyer escorts for convoys.

There were several major engagements between British and German vessels off the Dorset coast, and aircraft from Warmwell, which had fought so well during the Battle of Britain, continued to soar into the skies to challenge the enemy planes.

At the end of November 1942, my sister gave birth to a fine healthy boy, and our hearts were gladdened by the arrival of the first of a new generation of the family. In the spring of 1943, we had joyful confirmation that Dolores was expecting our own first child, due around November. Though the best beginning for a family may not be in time of war, we were determined to live our lives in the hope of better days ahead. In spite of the desperate times that prevailed, there were now hints of cautious optimism in the air. The Axis forces in Africa surrendered, and news came of the successful "Dambusters" raid by British Lancaster bombers on the Mohne and Eder dams in the Ruhr valley of Germany. The bouncing bomb idea of Barnes Wallace had first been tested out in the Fleet, behind the Chesil Beach near Weymouth.

In light of the fact that the position of the Italian dictator Mussolini was beginning to crumble, an incident which occurred during this period, when I was taking soldiers to the Breakwater Forts one day, was the more remarkable. As a couple of planes flew over us, everyone exclaimed with astonishment, for they bore Italian markings. Such planes had not, as far as I was aware, ventured into the Dorset area previously, although some had engaged in battles with our aircraft based in the south-east of England in the early part of the war. Luckily, the Italian planes dropped their bombs outside the Portland Harbour breakwater, where they did little damage. I have since heard that a soldier from the Dorsetshire Regiment, which fought in the Allied invasion of Italy, brought back with him a copy of an Italian newspaper documenting the bombing of Portland's sea defences by Italian aircraft.

The anxieties and hardships of the times probably contributed to the premature birth of our first daughter on 4 October 1943. Arriving home from duties, I found the midwife attending Dolores, but as was usual for husbands in those days, I was not very enlightened as to what was going on. When I was instructed to "Get the doctor quickly!" I ran to the nearest call box, deeply anxious for Dolores and her baby. On my return, I heard the anguished cries of my wife, and then suddenly the first cries of the little one. The midwife had coped well with a very difficult breech birth, and fortunately the child was small, weighing a little over five pounds. I was relieved and happy when I knew that Dolores and the baby were both safe after their ordeal.

With the invasion of Italy in full swing, it was now only a matter of time before the launch of the Second Front in Europe. Most people, including Hitler, assumed that an invading force would take the shortest sea route between the Kent coast and the area around Calais. The assumption was assiduously encouraged as preparations were made in Britain for the biggest operation of the whole war, and it seemed that nowhere along the south coast was the activity more intense than in Dorset.

There was a general feeling of tension and excitement as the pieces of the jigsaw began to fit into place, yet we dared not voice our opinions or hazard guesses, for the wartime slogan, "Careless talk costs lives", aptly highlighted the need for silence. Local people kept the biggest secret of all as realisation dawned that the coastlines of Hampshire and Dorset, not Kent, were to provide the main springboard for the liberation of Western Europe, and the beaches of Normandy were to be their target.

Leaving for D-Day, Weymouth Harbour June 1944.

The Dawn of D-Day

January 1944 was to bring a quickening of activity all over Dorset. Bolson's shipyard at Poole were building landing craft at a furious pace, while Weymouth Bay witnessed experiments with specially adapted scout cars, armoured cars and tanks, which could emerge from landing craft into five or six feet of water to make their way ashore. Floating roadways were also tried out in the bay. Weymouth and Portland became the base for the 14th Major Port of the Transportation Corps of the US Army. The numerous coastal forces craft comprising HMS *Bee*, which operated out of Weymouth Harbour during 1942 and well into 1943, had now made way for assault craft and other invasion vessels.

The pier at Castletown used by the Portland stone firms was adapted to provide a ramp for the loading of tanks and vehicles on to landing craft, and a vast marshalling yard was prepared at Ferrybridge. The woods, parks and country estates of Dorset concealed the gradual build-up of American troops in the county. US Army Air Force Lockheed Lightning planes were based at Warmwell Aerodrome and began bombing missions across the Channel. American jeeps and trucks careered around the highways and byways, causing considerable traffic problems. Road improvements had to be hastily carried out by the Americans, especially the widening of certain roads, including Ridgeway Hill near Weymouth, to accommodate the convoys that were converging on the town.

On 18 February, I was ordered to take *My Girl* to Poole for a major refit, and whilst this was in progress, I was assigned for some two months to the East Cowes Barracks and lodged at the Seamen's Mission at Cowes, Isle of Wight. Many sailors from the Free French Navy were quartered at the Mission at that time. All along the Dorset and Hampshire coast, fleets of landing craft were hidden away in creeks and inlets. Bailey Bridges, which had been developed at Christchurch, awaited the invasion call, and trials of PLUTO (Pipe Line Under the Ocean), which was to carry fuel direct to the Normandy coast, were carried out between Poole and the Isle of Wight. My new posting brought me into contact with some of the most important and urgent work of the war, for along with other War Department crew, I was working on the Mulberries, the top secret Allied project which was being assembled in the Solent.

The amazingly impressive creations known as the Mulberries were vital to the success of the invasion, and would be towed across the Channel immediately after D-Day to provide instant ports for the invading forces, one for the British troops and one for the Americans.

The Mulberry Harbours were giant floating boxes of concrete and steel, about 60 feet high, and were built to act as breakwaters and docking facilities, capable of rising and falling on the huge tides along the Normandy coastline.

Other prototypes, nicknamed "Spuds", were pontoons of articulated steel to provide roadways. These had 90 feet vertical steel columns, or "legs" at the four corners, which rested on the sea bed, while the level of the pontoons could be adjusted within the columns according to the tide. The concrete caissons, which were being produced at Southampton at a tremendous rate, were moored along the Solent, while the 'Spuds" were lined up between the Peel Bank and Ryde Pier.

Men of the Royal Engineers, drawn mostly from the London area, were maintaining and living aboard the Mulberries, on which cooking and other living facilities were provided. My task was to ferry men, stores and mail around the Mulberry Harbours which stretched from Wootton Creek on the Isle of Wight, out to the Peel Bank.

Opportunities for home leave with Dolores and our new baby during that busy period were rare, so in the few off-duty hours I had at my disposal, I rode the island's trains or went on walks to explore the countryside, the beauty and tranquillity of which enchanted me. I could understand now why Dolores retained a love for the island, which dated back to childhood holidays spent at the family home in Freshwater. I took the train one day to Ventnor and Sandown, but on my return to the railway station to get the last train, I discovered its final destination was Ryde, not Cowes.

Men are packed into landing craft like sardines in cans and must endure their cramped conditions even longer as bad weather puts back the D-Day departure. (Courtesy Weymouth Museum)

There followed a mad dash to try to get back to the Seamen's Mission before it closed for the night at ten o'clock. I hired a taxi to get me to the Cowes Ferry and we collected two sailors along the way who were also heading in the same direction. Our vehicle crept along like a snail in the blackout as the sound of gunfire drifted across the Solent from Portsmouth, where an air raid was obviously in progress. Fortunately, a ferry which had undergone repairs at East Cowes was ready to return to her moorings at West Cowes, and I was allowed to travel back on her. When I eventually reached the Mission, the front door was locked and barred against me. Now what was I to do?

After I had knocked on the door repeatedly and at length, the man in charge acknowledged me from the other side of the door. I identified myself and requested entry.

"I can't let you in. It's after ten," the man insisted. "It's more than my job's worth to open the door now!"

Although I had slept in the open air on many occasions in the past, I really did not fancy the idea on a cold spring night, especially when a bed was waiting for me inside. I noticed that a window on the first floor near to my quarters was still open, and there was an ancient, gnarled ivy growing up the wall to that level. It gave me an idea.

"Right, then," I said. "I shall climb up the ivy and get in that way."

I made as if to climb up the ivy, shaking it noisily. The front door of the Mission opened a fraction as the man peered out to see what I was up to. In a flash, I had my foot in the door, and slipping him half a crown to say no more about it, I slid safely inside.

In due course, the overhaul of *My Girl* was completed and after successful engine trials, we were back on station at Hope Quay and Bincleaves.

During those spring months, not without some casualties, mock invasion assaults had been carried out along the Dorset coasts. On the night of 28 April 1944, there occurred a tragedy of horrendous proportions which long remained shrouded in secrecy. That night, an American task force set out along the Channel en route for an Allied invasion exercise at Slapton Sands, Devon. The disaster which occurred during that exercise was cloaked in silence, and still provokes speculation to this day. By the following dawn, the bodies of hundreds of Americans were floating in the waters off Portland. In great haste, they were plucked from the sea, and many were brought ashore to Weymouth and Portland and spirited away, for it was vital that the Germans were not alerted to the fact that an invasion force was gathering in the south-west of Britain.

Only much later was it admitted that E-boats had come across the task force and opened fire on it. Rumours abounded to the effect that in the ensuing confusion, the Americans may have added to their own casualties by indiscriminate firing and ramming each other in the darkness. Whatever the truth, the incident resulted in the massacre of more than 600 young Americans. There was a feeling that if these men had been slaughtered by the Germans, they should have been honoured by Britain and America when the war ended, but there was never any mention of them. Even if there were blunders that night, these men were not destined for recognition similar to that accorded to the 600 who charged into the Valley of Death at another time, and in another place. It was only as a consequence of a determined effort by a few individuals that a memorial was erected at Slapton Sands in later years to the victims of this incident.

Life at Weymouth and Portland was busier than ever, and my duties now included ferrying the American pilots out to the landing craft moored in the harbours. The stores of provisions which also had to be conveyed included food, the like of which we had not seen in Britain for years. Some of the Americans perhaps felt embarrassed because they ate so well in a country where food was severely rationed. Certain it was that Freddie, our ship's boy, was allowed to take the odd tin of chicken, pineapple and other goodies home to his mother.

One of the happiest duties I had throughout the war years was to ferry the ENSA concert parties out to the forts to entertain the troops. For a little while, as the men sang along with the songs made popular by Vera Lynn, the "Forces' Sweetheart", they dreamed of the days to come when they would be reunited at home with their loved ones. The American servicemen were an ocean away from home, and many must have experienced times of homesickness. Some of the men had sweethearts in Weymouth, and those girls who married Americans later sailed to the USA as GI brides.

Orders came for me from the Transport Office to take out a special task force of about 20 Merchant Navy quartermasters for navigation lessons before the invasion. I set them compass courses for headlands which they had to steer to, such as Lulworth, Redcliff and White Nothe, while I monitored their accuracy. I also had the job of towing high-speed radio-controlled boats, known as "Queen Bees". These were about 12 feet long, decked in and painted bright red. Men from the Royal Engineers and Royal Signals aboard *My Girl* had radios tuned in to these boats which set them off unmanned, under remote control.

Along with a young Army officer, the Transport Office also instructed me to collect two new fast harbour launches built by Tods of Ferrybridge, and to undertake their sea trials. I took *My Girl* over to Ferrybridge with the captain and some crewmen to assist us, and we each took a launch out for its trials. The engines of the launches were sealed with a lead seal, and had a notice saying they were not to be used at full throttle until 50 hours running had been achieved.

Our boats were performing well when the captain drew alongside me. "Race you back to Weymouth!" he shouted.

He shot across the bay in his launch at a terrific rate of knots. His crew later said he had ripped off the seals from the engine of his vessel and opened her up at full speed. Apparently the temptation to try out the enormous power of such a fast launch was too much for him to resist. When I got into Weymouth Harbour, he had moored up and was long since gone. A few days later, Les Caddy, Bert Caddy, Charlie Bennett, Cyril Johnson and Frank Moggeridge, who comprised our trials crew, were ordered to take the launches to the Medina River at Cowes, Isle of Wight, ready for use by the British invasion forces.

By May 1944, we knew that the invasion was imminent. Weymouth and Portland Harbours were to be the departure points for the main American thrust across the Channel, while the British and Canadian troops were to sail from coasts further to the east. Whenever enemy raids were threatened, the Americans released smokescreens which drifted across the harbours and the town to mask the invasion preparations. The acrid stench of the smokescreen seemed to penetrate everything, and sometimes the whole of Weymouth was completely enveloped by thick, choking clouds. When raids actually occurred, the Americans tended to respond with great alacrity, so that shells and bullets flew through the blackout and smokescreens without any of us knowing quite where they would end up.

On 13 May, the pilot launch *Marina*, which was entering Portland Harbour against the signals, struck *My Girl* and caused her severe damage, with the result that she was on the Great Western Railway slipway in Weymouth until 21 May for repairs. In these days before electric winches, Bert Brown and I had to work the great winch by hand to haul her up the slipway.

Weymouth suffered a heavy air raid at the end of May, centred on the Melcombe Avenue area, which resulted in four deaths, many injuries and damage to some 400 houses. The local hospital was hit, and with a huge unexploded bomb deeply embedded in the ground nearby, patients had to be evacuated by the US Army to an emergency hospital in the local Weymouth College buildings.

June 4 saw the two harbours packed with landing craft and assault vessels. The loading of stores and ammunition went on at a frantic pace, that allowed little time for rest. The Royal and Edward Hotels in Weymouth, occupied by the Americans, were buzzing with activity. From all over Dorset, men of V Corps of the US Army came out of hiding and converged on Weymouth. Never before or since have the people of Weymouth witnessed such a spectacle, as thousands of soldiers descended on the town. The promenade was filled with the sight and sound of marching men. Tanks and armoured vehicles rumbled through the Wey Valley and headed to the marshalling area at Ferrybridge. When that was full, they parked nose to tail along the roadsides to await embarkation.

At dawn on 5 June, the air was charged with tension and expectation, but the D-Day orders had not yet come. Men were packed into landing craft like sardines in cans, and Weymouth Bay bustled with battleships, both British and American, waiting to bombard the French coast so as to soften up the enemy defences. Midget submarines had gone before them to clear areas near the beaches so that invasion craft could advance safely, for the Germans had earlier sunk steel spikes and traps below the water to prevent landings. When everything was ready for the invasion, all the preparations were suddenly disrupted by an enemy off our own coast: the weather. A south-westerly gale had blown up, the seas were rough, and it was bleak and miserable. The D-Day departure had to be put back one day.

For the troops penned up in the landing craft, the delay prolonged their ordeal as they waited, hungry and cold, in very cramped conditions. A small number were able to disembark and sat or stretched out on the promenade. Whilst they endured the postponement, some were apprehensive and thoughtful, others noisy and excited. All had been facing the most testing day in their lives, and that day was now lengthening into another. *My Girl* worked around the clock to get further supplies to the ships and to the forts. As we passed the loaded landing craft again and again, a few of the men aboard began to catcall and throw the last of their English coins at the boat. We took this in good part, for who could blame them for becoming restless when they were encased in coffin-like structures to wait on the whims of the British weather?

Throughout the night of 5-6 June, *My Girl* remained on active duty. The weather eased, and just after midnight, there came forth a galaxy of planes crossing the sky. Hundreds of bombers towing gliders passed overhead for several hours, carrying men and equipment to Normandy. My neck ached as I watched wave after wave of aircraft pass above me, and I knew this was D-Day. The American armada had also departed for Omaha Beach, and Weymouth and Portland Harbours were suddenly quiet as the frantic activity of the last few days ceased. Further west, other American troops had set out for Utah Beach, while to the east the British and Canadian forces had sailed for Gold, Juno and Sword Beaches. Exhausted but excited, we watched and waited for news.

The planes and gliders I had seen departing for Normandy had come from Tarrant Rushton Aerodrome in Dorset, and the men they carried were to secure their objectives. After the landings, the British and Canadian invasion troops forged ahead in their sectors, but the American Task Force O from Weymouth was to encounter the bloodiest fighting of the whole invasion upon Omaha Beach. For many hours, their assault seemed to be on the very brink of disaster. The men had arrived at Omaha Beach seasick and wet through after a rough crossing in flat-bottomed boats. Tanks and guns were lost in heavy seas, and soldiers were thrown into the water when their landing craft sank. The softening up bombardment by planes and battleships overshot the German defences, leaving them intact, and it ended prematurely when low cloud settled over the area. The men waded ashore, up to their necks in water, to find themselves in minefields in which they met a hail of machine-gun fire, without the protection of the tanks which should have gone in before them. Despite terrible losses and injuries, the men of V Corps fought heroically and managed to take the beach for the Allies.

In the aftermath of D-Day, the 14th Major Port of the Transportation Corps of the US Army continued to send further waves of troops from Weymouth to Normandy, from whence vessels returned with large numbers of wounded men for treatment in the US Army hospitals which had been set up in Dorset. The skies over the Channel remained busy as aircraft supported Allied shipping and undertook raids into France. The Mulberry Harbours were soon operating successfully, although the artificial port set up for the

Americans was wrecked in a fierce gale later in June and all vehicles and tanks had to be sent in via the British harbour. The invasion of Normandy also resulted in the capture of German rocket sites on that coast, sparing our coast from attacks similar to those that had been suffered in the London area the previous autumn. The severe equinoxial gales of that year also added to the wartime casualty list when an American tank landing craft was thrown on to the Chesil Beach by huge seas, and 12 men were drowned, despite brave attempts to save them.

The anniversary in November of the First World War armistice of 1918 marked the birth of our first son. As we celebrated the safe and welcome arrival of my namesake, we continued to hope for a better and brighter world ahead for our little ones. Our housing conditions were very poor, for we occupied upstairs rooms in an older house in the Rodwell area of Weymouth, and shared the bathroom facilities with the very temperamental landlord who lived below. There was no kitchen; one room had an old gas cooker in one corner, and crockery and pots and pans had to be stacked under the table. All the washing and the washing-up had to be done in the bathroom. A welcome escape from our cramped and difficult living conditions was provided by the public gardens at The Nothe and Sandsfoot, where we spent many hours walking together, and pushing the babies in their pram.

As the Allies kept up their offensive, the main theatre of war moved deeper into Europe, although the harbours of Weymouth and Portland were still busy. Day in and day out, *My Girl* continued to plough between the forts, battleships and quays with servicemen, stores and equipment. It almost seemed as if she was capable of sailing herself around the course, so well did she know it by then. As for me, I lost count of the numbers of men, including high-ranking British and American officers, whom I had transported.

The close of 1944 witnessed the German Ardennes offensive, in which the Luftwaffe was greatly outnumbered by Allied bombers and fighter planes. Despite the advances of the Allies, and the bombing raids which pounded the German cities, Hitler would not accept the inevitable, thus prolonging the war. In March, the Ludendorff Bridge over the Rhine fell into Allied hands, providing the starting point for the attack on the Ruhr and climaxing in the surrender of German troops in the area in April. The race for Berlin was now on. By 4 May, Hitler had committed suicide and a surrender document was signed and a ceasefire declared on 5 May. Now the gas masks could finally be put away and the blackout blinds removed, along with the criss-cross tapes on window panes that were optimistically intended to diminish the danger from flying broken glass in bomb explosions. VE Day was celebrated on 8 May 1945 with tea parties in the streets and church bells ringing throughout the land to mark the victory. The war in Europe was over at last.

A day or so after the end of the war, the first German U-boat to surrender came into Portland Harbour. The officer at the Transport Office instructed me to proceed with *My Girl* to pick up a party of ATS girls at Bincleaves and soldiers from the Breakwater Forts, and take them to view the submarine. The next day, two further German submarines arrived, one in Portland, the other in Weymouth; and a fourth one arrived from the Isle of Wight some days later.

For the Americans, having diverted their energies into ending the war with Japan, their task at Weymouth and Portland was over. A memorial to the American servicemen stands on the Promenade at Weymouth opposite the Royal Hotel, and a plaque at Portland has the inscription:

> *The major part of the American Assault Force which landed on the shores of France 6 June 1944 was launched from Weymouth and Portland Harbors. From 6 June 1944 to 7 May 1945, 517,816 troops and 144,093 vehicles embarked from these Harbors. Many of these vehicles left Weymouth Pier. The remainder of the troops and all vehicles passed through Weymouth en route to Portland points of embarkation.*
>
> *Presented by the 14th Major Port, US Army.*
> *Harold G. Miller, Major, T.C. Sub Port Commander.*
> *Sherman L. Kiser, Colonel, T.C. Port Commander.*

Few other signs now remain in this area of the presence of the American forces, but we were very thankful they had come to stand beside us in the darkest days of the war. Without them, the struggle to win the war would surely have been a long and bleak one. Indeed the courage and sacrifices of all service personnel and civilians alike should be remembered. For my own part, I was truly glad to have completed my duties as skipper aboard *My Girl* without incurring the loss of a single life out of all the many passengers I was entrusted with over those years.

Gradually the forts were being run down, and many of the soldiers who had manned them had been posted to the Channel Islands following their liberation from German occupation. The long-standing links between Weymouth and the islands were slowly restored as the Channel Islands steamers returned from war duties. Britain was also looking to finish the war with Japan. One particular task allocated to me and several other War Department crewmen was to ferry two large motor launches from Portland to Hampton, on the River Thames, for refitting prior to their shipment to the Far East.

The first part of our journey along the coast in the launches was quite difficult, because the weather was very foggy, and we also had to keep a lookout for mines which still posed a real danger in the Channel. Later on the weather improved, and as we passed Beachy Head, I looked up to the top of those sheer heights to glimpse the tail of one of our planes overhanging the very edge of the cliffs, looking as if it had literally only just made it back across the Channel.

We had permission to moor the launches overnight in the Dover Pens, and proceeded to London the next day. After we had reported our arrival at Woolwich, something of a race developed between our two vessels, for we had been informed that the first crew reaching our destination could return home, leaving the other to take charge of both launches until they were formally handed over. As we proceeded higher up the river, negotiating locks and passing the little islands in the Thames, the waterway became progressively narrow and shallow. In those leisurely reaches, our crewmen spotted a rowing boat with three attractive young girls aboard, and we were all so busy waving to them that we failed to realise the effect our wash was having in the confines of the river. As we sped past the girls and glanced back to give them a final wave, we saw to our horror that our wake had hit the riverbank and rebounded, and was now advancing on their little craft. The more frantically we signalled to warn the girls, the more enthusiastically they waved back at us, blissfully unaware of the threatening danger. All at once, their boat was carried along like a surfboard at Bondi Beach, and they were deposited high on the muddy bank of one of the islands. Fortunately, they did not capsize, but even from a distance, we could see that they were none too pleased at their predicament. Having ascertained that they were unharmed, we decided to scarper pretty smartly, rather than face their wrath. They obviously lodged a complaint about us, because we were later admonished by a lock keeper for upsetting the whole of the upper river with our race, having failed to appreciate that a speed limit of three or four miles per hour was in force.

On my return to Weymouth after my London trip, I was devastated to discover that *My Girl* had been taken out by the crew member detailed to act as caretaker while I was away, and that she had been in collision with part of the breakwater and suffered a fire in her engine. I was kept busy during the whole of the following week on repairs and clearing up operations.

The end of War Department duties for *My Girl* was now in sight. Her job was done and I made my final entries in her log as follows:

24.7.45 Proceeded to Cowes, Isle of Wight, towing WDV *Grenadier*.

25.7.45 To Victoria Jetty, towing *Grenadier*.

26.7.45 Victoria Barracks, Cowes. Inventory and unloading equipment. RASC moorings.

27.7.45 To Poole, Bolson's Shipyard, towing *Grenadier*.

30.7.45 Handover of *My Girl*, *Grenadier*, *Alouette* and *Sea Kestrel* with equipment.

31.7.45 Crew to Cowes, No.3 Section, 615 Water Transport Company, RASC.

1.8.45 Took over WDV *Estella*.

The handover of *My Girl* was an emotional moment. Along with other War Department vessels, she was to be laid up, and I had no idea how long it would be before I saw her again, or when we would be given the opportunity to buy her back. She had served both me and her country well, but for the time being, I had to bid her farewell, and it was a sad parting.

However, there was little time to dwell on such thoughts, for I had to take over the *Estella*, a cabin cruiser in service with the Solent Section of 635 Water Transport Company.

The release of atomic bombs on Hiroshima and Nagasaki in August 1945 marked the arrival of the nuclear age and the conclusion of the war with Japan. Now that the Second World War was truly at an end, I began to wonder what the future held for me.

4/5 June 1944. Loading landing craft; at Castletown, Portland.
The Harbour and Weymouth Bay beyond bristle with warships
which will bombard the French coast to soften up the enemy
defences prior to the arrival of the invasion force.
(Courtesy Geoffrey Carter)

Beginning Again

By January 1946, I had been travelling daily between Weymouth and Poole for several months. As Mate in Charge of LCT 887, my job involved taking her between Poole, Sandbanks, Brownsea Island and Green Island, ferrying parties of soldiers to the forts in the area to commence stripping down the guns and dismantling the minefields. Old ammunition and smoke bombs from the South Coast defences were eventually taken out to the Hurd Deep by the vessel *Peter Joliffe* and dumped into the sea. Another of my duties entailed making postal deliveries between the islands of Poole Harbour, and this included taking mail to Mrs Mary Florence Bonham-Christie, who lived as a recluse in Brownsea Castle. I sometimes ferried her son, Major Christie, on visits to see his mother. I was offered a position as ferryman/caretaker on the island, but I declined, knowing that Brownsea at the time was populated by colonies of rats and mosquitoes.

That period was a time of difficult decisions in my life, all of which hinged to a very great extent on the War Department, and when invited to apply for discharge, I did so and this was eventually granted. There seemed to be no prospect of my returning to Plymouth to re-establish myself there, since the housing situation in that war-torn city was even more desperate than that which existed in Weymouth. I had just to remain where I was and try to start to earn a living in the pleasure boat business in Weymouth, despite the fact that the conditions in the upstairs rooms where we lived were still quite dreadful. Although we now had three children and were under notice to quit, the prospects of rehousing were a long way off. All my searches for other rented accommodation failed to bear fruit; there was absolutely nothing available in the town. However, in the euphoria that existed in the immediate post-war era, we trusted that the tomorrow we had worked and waited for was going to be a better day. Hadn't we all believed it when Vera Lynn sang of the bluebirds over the white cliffs of Dover?

I was notified that I was eligible to receive the Atlantic Medal for my war service, and my hopes were pinned on the fact that our situation would be eased when my gratuity came through.

With luck, it would enable Father and me to buy back *My Girl* when the War Department released her, and there might even be a little left over to put towards a home of our own.

My dreams that life was going to be easier once the war was over were to prove to have been sadly misplaced, for in the end, no gratuity payment was forthcoming for me. My correspondence over the matter went to and from the two Transport Offices under whose command I had been, but neither seemed able to resolve the issue for me. Months passed by and my application disappeared somewhere in the vast machinery of the War Department, which was coping with the discharge of many men, and it never came to light again. As I handed in my service uniform with its gold braid denoting the rank of Lieutenant, I felt very disillusioned, as others had received their gratuities in full. That setback was a bitter blow, but there was nothing else for it than to pick myself up and begin my life all over again.

After my discharge, I travelled daily to J. Bolson's shipyard at Poole and set to work on *My Girl*, stripping off all the old grey paint, rubbing down, sandpapering and repainting, varnishing and anti-fouling, awaiting the day when she could be bought back from the Government. That day came in the summer of 1946, and Father travelled from Plymouth and we journeyed to Poole, where the purchase money was handed over and a bill for repair work was paid. Then we took in fuel and brought her back to Weymouth, tying up at Hope Quay. How great was my joy that *My Girl* was ours again! Her white paint glistened in the sunlight, the cabin and seats were beautifully varnished and her name boards enhanced with gold leaf. She was now ready to resume her role of bringing pleasure to holidaymakers eager for a boat trip along the coast.

Father returned to Plymouth, still hopeful that I would be able to follow in due course. In the meantime, since I had quickly to establish some means to support my little family in Weymouth, I applied for permission to run *My Girl* from Weymouth Harbour. I had already obtained a Board of Trade certificate while at Poole and requested the necessary ration coupons for fuel to run the boat. I felt sure that with hard work, I would be able to surmount my difficulties and eventually obtain a house with a garden for the children. There was the possibility of renewing my links with the coach drivers who before the war had brought their passengers to the quayside in Plymouth for trips in *My Girl*. I knew the drivers from all the big companies, and they would surely be coming again to Weymouth. The future began to look a little rosier.

Nothing was going to be easy for me. Apparently there were rules and regulations preventing me from running from Weymouth Harbour, in spite of the fact that *My Girl* had worked throughout the war contributing to the defence of that harbour. In desperation, I asked for permission to run *My Girl* from the open beach, although this would present enormous difficulties if winds freshened from the east, and when tides receded and made the landing of passengers almost impossible. After long drawn-out negotiations, I was eventually allocated a pitch to the south side of the Pier Bandstand. There, Bert Brown joined me as able seaman, and with a short length of staging, I set out on my venture.

I had anticipated that there would be problems, and this assumption was soon proved right. Without a landing jetty, passengers had to be rowed out from the shore by dinghy and put aboard *My Girl* about ten at a time. I later acquired a flat-bottomed punt for this purpose.

On the return journey, I often had to contend with a fast-receding tide, which necessitated bringing the boat in as near to the beach as I dared, and off-loading people into the dinghy or punt and ferrying them ashore.

Our passengers were truly wonderful. It seemed that after years of wartime restrictions, people were determined to enjoy their new-found freedom. Many paddled the last ten feet or so through the shallows; men rolled up their trousers, women hitched up their skirts, carried their shoes and waded ashore, laughing and joking as they went. I had to carry the older folk to shore then dash back quickly to *My Girl* to ensure she didn't go aground before the next passengers lined up for a trip.

The course previously sailed by the boat on war service now became an hour's pleasure cruise, taking in Weymouth Bay and the whole of Portland Harbour, viewing the warships, sea defences and sections of the Mulberry Harbours which had played such a vital role in ensuring the success of the D-Day landings. Portland Harbour, which had been established as a training base for the British Navy, was usually filled by an impressive array of aircraft carriers, battleships, destroyers, frigates and submarines. Along with *Vanguard* and *Victorious*, great ships such as *Illustrious*, *Implacable* and *Indefatigable* were based there. American ships were frequent visitors, amongst them the mighty battleship *Missouri* and the aircraft carrier *F.D. Roosevelt*.

With such a strong naval presence in the area, the local taverns prospered. Weymouth was reputed to have a pub on every street corner, and they all did a roaring trade when the fleet was in.

At long last, in the summer of 1947, our housing problem was resolved when we were allocated a council house on the outskirts of the town. There, despite the shortages of furniture and household equipment of every kind, Dolores and I established the first real home of our own, in the house which was to remain home for us and our five children for many years. While new house building, repair and conversion gradually eased the situation for other families who had endured conditions similar to ours, the terrible scars of bombing raids were long to remain in certain areas of the town, notably Chapelhay. The heavy cost of the war was still being felt as the rationing of food, clothing and fuel lingered on and on.

In the aftermath of the war, when people longed to escape to the seaside for a well-deserved break, Weymouth returned to favour as a family holiday resort. Motor coaches filled with day trippers crowded into Westham coach park, and steam trains disgorged their passengers into King Street each Saturday, the holiday population reaching its peak during Swindon Week, when the workers of that railway town took their annual leave.

On warm, sunny days, the seashore was so thronged with people that scarcely a patch of sand or pebbles on the beach remained unfilled. Beach stalls sold ice cream and jugs of tea, along with beach balls, water wings and brightly enamelled buckets and spades. Throughout such days, a great wave of sound rose continuously into the air; the happy expression of thousands of people at play upon that golden shore.

Other boatmen soon came to join me on the seafront, and during the peak years of the trade, four other launches ran with *My Girl* in the pleasure boat business, trading as White Motor Boats. Cosens and Co. also ran launches from a site by the Jubilee Clock on the Esplanade, in addition to their fleet of paddle steamers, which operated from the Pier. We were gradually able to afford more staging and a string of pontoons to assist in the embarkation of passengers. The pontoons were towed daily to and from Weymouth Harbour, and anchored in position. Although they eased matters in one direction, they brought problems in other ways, for the smallest changes in the weather required immediate action to re-lay anchors and re-adjust the moorings of our boats. Sudden swings in wind direction or unexpected sea swells, such as occurred after high speed manoeuvres by ships of the Royal Navy, had to be watched for and responded to at once.

Our fickle climate also meant that there were summers when the days were wet and cold, or the wind swung to the east and stubbornly remained there, preventing us from working for days or even weeks at a time. As those days ticked by, I could only kick my heels and watch and wait for the weather to change. I had to live from one summer to the next, hoping to earn enough money in those fleeting weeks to help tide me through the long winter months; and a poor season meant that real hardship lay ahead.

Out of season, I had to take any work I could find, as I had no boat of my own in Weymouth suitable for fishing at that time. I was soon to link up again with Vic Charles of Portland, and together we went trawling in his small boat during the long winter nights in the difficult waters around Portland and West Bay. My ears became attuned to the moods of the Chesil and our proximity to it in the darkness. The gentle swish and sigh of the sea upon the pebbles in calmer moments could quickly give way to a more menacing and sinister growl with the onset of bad weather. One night, in difficult conditions, we almost ran upon the bank, being warned just in time of our dangerous situation by a million phosphorescent lights dancing in the waters breaking on the edge of the beach.

Stormy weather brought about numerous calls on the Weymouth lifeboat *William and Clara Ryland*, and it was an honour to crew aboard her on rescue work, and also to assist with the deliveries of vessels to lifeboat stations and ship repair yards around the coast. It was a privilege at that time to serve with and learn from the much respected lifeboatmen, Joe Vine and Fred Palmer. We experienced some very testing missions, for inshore waters such as the Dorset coast are often more treacherous than the middle of mighty oceans, a fact that many weekend yachtsmen discover to their cost.

In addition to trawling during the winter, I turned my hand to tree felling, yacht ferrying and maintenance, laying the Sailing Club moorings in Weymouth and refitting work on the Channel Island vessels. My various painting assignments took me from the dark bowels of ships to the tops of the crane jibs on the quayside, where the view from aloft was as breathtaking as the icy wind blowing across the harbour.

I was at hand one day when a lad of about 12, on holiday with his parents in Weymouth, wandered off and climbed to the top of one of the cranes. He became stuck there, too frightened to move, but fortunately I was able to climb up after him and gently coax him down. On one occasion, while I was working on the cranes, I took my camera along with me and gained some original photographs of the harbour from my perch at the top of the jib.

Some more unusual views of Weymouth came about one summer when the spire of St John's church was undergoing repairs. I negotiated the network of scaffolding and ladders to join the steeplejack, and captured the wonderful panorama of the bay below me. As I was busy clicking away, the Rector chanced to spot me as he was walking in the gardens adjoining the church, and he shouted and waved to me to come down at once. I made my way down the scaffolding and jumped the last ten feet or so of the descent, well out of sight of the bottom of the ladder, where he awaited my arrival in vain.

Within a few years, Father handed over to me the keeping of the little fishing boat *Wee Hee*, and I brought her from Plymouth and moored her beside *My Girl*. The second arrival at Weymouth of *Wee Hee* brings my story full circle, for she then became my partner during the winter months until the days lengthened again and it was time to prepare *My Girl* for another holiday season.

As the summer seasons waxed and waned, one of my greatest pleasures was to greet old friends who came back year after year for trips in *My Girl*. Many of them were soldiers who had manned the Weymouth and Portland sea defences during the war, returning with their wives and children for holidays in the town. Remembering the dangers of the journeys, we had shared together under gunfire and bombing, their trips were always without charge.

At the close down of the forts at the end of hostilities, the men of the Royal Artillery gave me as a keepsake their flag, which I treasured until, sadly, it finally fell to pieces. Memories of those wartime days continue to flood back whenever I open the five volumes which represent an enduring testament to *My Girl*, the original log books kept during those troubled times.

Many years have now elapsed since the outbreak of the Second World War and the arrival of *My Girl* in Weymouth. Some of the many brave people she carried on their mission to defeat the enemy who would enslave our nation are still living, and will have fond memories of her as a War Department craft, in her working coat of sombre grey. It is thanks to them and all who joined them in the defeat of Hitler that she was able to return to her peaceful task of providing pleasure for free people on carefree days off Dorset's lovely coast.

They will surely be delighted to know that after all this time, back in her livery of white, she is still setting out on summer days from her berth at Weymouth, laden with happy passengers aboard.

It is also a tribute to the men who designed and built her that she survived all the rigours of war service and remains to this day the fine craft she has always been. They built her strong, and they built her to last. They gave me a boat that I could trust and depend on for the safety of all who sailed in her.

A boat that is still my pride and joy.

On her war service, *My Girl* carried men and women of every rank, from generals to, in John Masefield's words, "the men hemmed in with the spears" who formed the bulk of her passengers.

It is to John Masefield, the poet to whose treasure house I was led by the woman I fell in love with, that I turn for a fitting epilogue to my story:

Consecration

Not of the princes and prelates with periwigged charioteers
Riding triumphantly laurelled to lap the fat of the years,
Rather the scorned - the rejected - the men hemmed in with the
  spears;

The men of the tattered battalion which fights till it dies,
Dazed with the dust of the battle, the din and the cries,
The men with the broken heads and the blood running into their
  eyes;

Not the bemedalled Commander, beloved of the throne,
Riding cock-horse to parade when the bugles are blown,
But the lads who carried the Koppie and cannot be known.

Not the ruler for me, but the ranker, the tramp of the road,
The slave with the sack on his shoulders pricked on with the goad,
The man with too weighty a burden, too weary a load.

The sailor, the stoker of steamers, the man with the clout,
The chantyman bent at the halliards putting a tune to the shout,
The drowsy man at the wheel and the tired look-out.

Others may sing of the wine and the wealth and the mirth,
The portly presence of potentates goodly in girth
Mine be the dirt and the dross,the dust and scum of the earth!

Theirs be the music, the colour, the glory, the gold;
Mine be a handful of ashes, a mouthful of mould.
Of the maimed, of the halt and the blind in the rain and the cold

Of these shall my songs be fashioned, my tales be told.

Amen.

Passengers landing after an hour's cruise in the 1950s, viewing Weymouth Bay, the Breakwater Forts, Portland Harbour and the warships anchored there. The landing area and pontoons were adjacent to the Pier Bandstand on Weymouth's Esplanade for many years before relocation to Brewer's Quay. (Author's Collection)

EPILOGUE TO WEYMOUTH AT WAR – UPDATED 2016

As the daughter of Ron Hill, it was my privilege during his retirement through illness, to record my father's experiences as a mariner, including his years with his beloved *My Girl*.

Ron was born in Plymouth, and his seafaring memories spanned an era of sail from the beautiful J-Class yachts which raced in Plymouth Sound in the early twentieth century, to the World Windspeed Championships, an event held regularly in Portland Harbour since the 1970s. Tim Colman, owner of the famous world record breaking yachts *Crossbow* and *Crossbow II*, attributed his successive victories over the years to Ron's superb seamanship and expert knowledge of conditions in that area.

Ron and his wife Dolores were a devoted couple, who successfully raised their five children, and enjoyed their seven grandchildren. Their years were not without sadness, however, as Bert Hill died in 1967, having never fully recovered from his wartime injury, and their son John, who also became skipper of *My Girl*, died in 1982 after a long illness. The vessel then passed into the care of Skipper Ian Robertson and his wife Irene (formerly Hill), and Ron continued to work with his new, smaller boat *Amigo*, until illness forced his retirement.

Presentation of RAA Pennant to *My Girl* in 1994 by Major General Steele (pictured first left), M. Agent (second left) and R. Pitman (far right), both Retired RA soldiers, Skipper Ian Robertson (third left), Marian Lye (centre) and Irene Robertson (second right). (Courtesy of Ian and Irene Robertson)

During the early 1990s, the deaths of Ron and Dolores, within eight months of each other, were times of immense sorrow, but they left behind a legacy of many happy memories for their family. Sight of the 1990 publication of the first edition of *Weymouth at War* had brought them both great pleasure.

In 1994, *My Girl* was honoured by the presentation of the pennant of the Royal Artillery Association by Major General Steele. Ron would have been very proud to see this flag fluttering from *My Girl's* flagstaff. The vessel was also accorded membership of The Historic Fleet of the United Kingdom.

My Girl later went into the safe hands of Paul Compton of Weymouth, the highly regarded Tall Ships Master. The vessel is now owned by Peter Broatch of Coastline Cruises, Weymouth. During a major refit, Peter Broatch has lovingly restored *My Girl*, enabling her to return to the waterfront at Weymouth Harbour alongside her companion *Enchantress*, and to welcome aboard friends old and new.

M.L.

Wee Hee stormbound in Weymouth Harbour, September 1937, after her voyage from the Channel Islands. (Author's Collection)

Home Guards at The Nothe, undertaking target practice with Lee-Enfield rifles. The shoreline of Weymouth Bay, visible in the background, was barricaded during the war years. (Courtesy Nothe Fort Museum)

My Girl preparing to embark soldiers eager for leave from the cramped conditions of the Portland Breakwater Forts. The vessel is pictured in the early part of the war, still painted overall in white, and prior to the building of the cabin. (Courtesy Nothe Fort Museum)

Ron Hill aboard *My Girl* at Hope Quay, preparing for another day's duties conveying men and stores to the Portland Breakwater Forts. (Author's Collection)

Billy Brown and Albert Holland, crew members of *My Girl*, at Hope Quay, Weymouth. (Author's Collection)

My Girl at Hope Quay, Weymouth, with crew members Cyril Johnson and Nelson Smith. The frame attached to the mast carries identification lights which had to be shown by vessels during the war. (Author's Collection)

Heavy seas crashing over the Stone Pier at the entrance to
Weymouth Harbour. In storm conditions, with a full complement
of men and stores, rounding the Stone Pier with *My Girl* was
a hazardous and uncomfortable experience.
(Courtesy Weymouth Museum)

The Weymouth Lifeboat, *William and Clara Ryland*. She
undertook many wartime rescues, including those which
followed attacks on shipping, and to search for pilots whose
planes had ditched into the sea. (Courtesy Weymouth Museum)

The Lifeboat Crew, including James MacDermott ("Mac"), seated left with his dog, Bruce. It was a great privilege to serve alongside these brave men, on occasions during and after the war. (Courtesy Weymouth Museum)

The Breakwater from Bincleaves. During a fierce air attack in August 1940, pieces of shrapnel embedded themselves in the timbers of *My Girl* when the nearby Shipwright's Store received a direct hit. A German machine gunner also attempted to mow down a butcher's boy returning along the Breakwater after delivering goods to HMS Vernon, the Torpedo Depot, shown near top left. (Courtesy Geoffrey Carter)

The Breakwater Lighthouse and East Ship Channel to Portland Harbour. *My Girl* experienced a close encounter with a drifting mine near this Breakwater.
(Courtesy HMS Osprey Photographic Unit)

My Girl regularly supplied the forts with consignments of the half-hundredweight shells for the six-inch guns. When the big guns opened up, the noise was deafening. (Courtesy Geoffrey Carter)

Bombs falling over the Chequered Fort, Portland Harbour.
An unusual raid on the harbour was carried out by planes bearing
Italian markings. Fortunately, the bombs released by those aircraft
fell into the sea outside the Breakwater and caused no damage.
(Courtesy Geoffrey Carter)

MERCHANT NAVY A/A GUNNERY COURSE.

TWO DAY COURSE
CERTIFICATE OF PROFICIENCY.

Name ........R.B. Hill..

Rank or Rating.........Mate...

B. of T. or D.B. No...........W.K.C.1222821..............................

has completed the Merchant Navy A/A Gunnery

Course and is qualified in the firing and cleaning

and oiling of *...Lewis, Hotchkiss, Marlin, .5....

Browning Colt, Oerlikon, F.A.M.,F.A.C., 2" Rocket

Rank ....Lieut. Commander, R.N.......

D.E.M.S.
Training Centre.............SOUTHAMPTON..........

* Insert types of guns and/or A/A devices.

(636) Wt. 9947/P5754 30M 5/43 S.E.R. Ltd. Gp. 671   (OVER

War Department boat crew were required to undertake gunnery
courses at regular intervals. This Certificate of Proficiency was
issued in 1943 following a two-day course at Southampton.
(Author's Collection)

Following a savage raid by German aircraft on the morning of 4 July 1940, HMS *Foylebank* burns fiercely. Leading Seaman Jack Mantle continued to fire the starboard gun, although mortally wounded, and was posthumously awarded the Victoria Cross for his bravery. (Courtesy Weymouth Museum)

A dark pall of smoke drifts across Portland Harbour as HMS *Foylebank* sinks. Jack Mantle, VC, lies buried in the cemetery overlooking Portland Harbour. (Courtesy Geoffrey Carter)

HMS *Foylebank* before her conversion into an anti-aircraft ship. 143 men died in the raid of 4 July 1940. (Courtesy Weymouth Museum)

The Royal Adelaide Hotel, Westham, Weymouth, November 1941.
Mayor John Goddard was trapped in the ruins of his home for
several hours but eventually emerged unscathed. Note the Union
Jack fluttering defiantly from the rafters.

Devastation at the Bus Depot, Weymouth, on the morning after
a bombing raid in October 1940.

Work commences on clearing up at Newstead Road, Weymouth, August 1940, after three houses were totally destroyed and the remainder badly damaged.
(Pictures courtesy Weymouth Museum)

The delicate task of raising and de-activating this unexploded bomb was to last for a week. The bomb had embedded itself some 28 feet into the ground near the hospital.
(Pictures courtesy Weymouth Museum)

The friendly invasion of Weymouth

The emblem of the 14th Major Port of the Transportation Corps of the United States Army - a familiar sight in Weymouth, and also in Poole and Southampton.

(Picture courtesy Rodney Legg's
Dorset at War: Diary of WW2)

Coffee and doughnuts for the American troops, June 1944.
This refreshment post was provided on the Esplanade at
Greenhill, Weymouth. (Courtesy Weymouth Museum)

(Courtesy Weymouth Museum)

Weymouth Harbour 4/5 June 1944. D-Day preparations are in full swing as thousands of American soldiers file aboard landing craft. (Pictures courtesy Weymouth Museum)

4/5 June 1944. Loading of troops and stores at Weymouth Quay.
Men are packed into landing craft like sardines in cans and
must endure their cramped conditions even longer as
bad weather puts back the D-Day departure.
(Pictures courtesy Weymouth Museum)

4/5 June 1944. Vehicles rumbled through Weymouth and headed for the marshalling area at Ferrybridge. When that was full, they parked nose to tail along the Chesil Beach road. (Pictures courtesy Weymouth Museum)

4/5 June 1944. Loading tank landing craft at Castletown, Portland. Portland Harbour and Weymouth Bay beyond bristle with warships which will bombard the French coast to soften up the enemy defences prior to the arrival of the invasion force. (Courtesy Geoffrey Carter)

4/5 June 1944. From the marshalling areas the trucks backed on to the landing craft at Castletown, Portland.
(Pictures courtesy Weymouth Museum)

10 May 1945. The first German U-boat to surrender is escorted into Weymouth Bay. (Courtesy Weymouth Museum)

View of the Chequered Fort in peacetime, with Portland in the background. (Courtesy of HMS Osprey Photographic Section)

Happy days are here again! The war is over and *My Girl* sets out for a pleasure cruise to Portland Harbour with carefree holidaymakers aboard.

Ron Hill (centre), with crew, pictured on Weymouth Esplanade close to the summer base for *My Girl* and the White Motor Boats. (Author's Collection)

The base for *My Girl* and the White Motor Boats was for many years adjacent to the Pier Bandstand on the Esplanade at Weymouth. Now, the Coastline Cruises base for *My Girl* and *Enchantress* is at Brewers Quay, Weymouth.
(Author's Collection)

Ron and Dolores Hill, pictured at the door of their
first home in 1942. (Author's Collection)

THE LANDMARK WALKS

We often retrace the landmark walks we made as children, with our parents Ron and Dolores Hill, around the shoreline of Weymouth and Portland. The three walks described are set out as Timewalks, so, if you care to follow in our footsteps, you will discover more of the history of the area, including the huge role played in World War 2 by the small ports of Weymouth and Castletown in the epic events that began the liberation of Europe. You will also enjoy an area of great natural beauty, including views of the world famous Jurassic Coastline and the two harbours, and you can experience some of the more recent amenities which have been developed along the way.

Many of the locations referred to in these walks are pictured within the pages of *Weymouth at War: Ron Hill's story of the vessel "My Girl"*. Key photographic references are indicated during the walks.

WALK 1: THE ESPLANADE WALK -

from Greenhill Gardens to Weymouth Harbourside.

Commencing beside Greenhill Gardens on the Esplanade, the spectacular sea views at this point take in the lovely sweep of Weymouth Bay, framed by the hills and white cliffs of the Jurassic Coast. Keep the sea on your left, and walk down the Esplanade, bounded by its Georgian terraces, towards Weymouth Harbour. To the south, the high ground of The Nothe Promontory will be visible, together with the newer landmark of the Skyline Tower, which provides a gull's eye view of the whole area.

Imagine this area on 4/5 June 1944. The bay was filled with ships preparing to depart for the French Coast. The beach was barricaded, and contingents of American soldiers were marching down the Esplanade. The troops paused at Greenhill, for coffee and doughnuts (opposite), served from a makeshift tent, before marching on towards Weymouth Harbour, where flotillas of landing craft waited to take them to Omaha Beach on D-Day.

Their route, and yours, leads past Weymouth's War Memorials. The first is the memorial to the local men who fell in two World Wars, and the Anzac War Memorial stands close by. Proceed to the Jubilee Clock Tower, commemorating the 50th anniversary of Queen Victoria's reign, and pause for a moment in front of the Royal Hotel, where the American World War 2 Memorial stands, dedicated to the many who left this shoreline and died in the battle to liberate Europe. The walk now takes you to the Statue of King George III, who spent holidays in Weymouth with his family for many summers from 1789. George brought the Royal Court with him on his visits, and made the town fashionable and famous.

Coffee and doughnuts for the American troops, June 1944. This refreshment post was provided on the Esplanade at Greenhill, Weymouth. (Courtesy Weymouth Museum)

Walk for another few minutes towards York Buildings, the first terrace of houses built in 1783 to face the sea. This has become a favoured area for sitting out at tea shops and cafes. You might like to rest awhile at this point, to enjoy some tea and a view of the sea, and, perhaps, contemplate the drama played out here in 1944. The little tea shop named "The Tea Bush" (with the bow window in the centre of this 1783 terrace) will delight you with homemade Dorset cream teas and apple cake. Its customers say they are "simply the best!"

Continue your journey towards the Pavilion Theatre, which occupies the site of the former wooden Pavilion Theatre (known later as the Ritz Theatre), which was destroyed by fire in the 1950s. Here, in June 1944, the whole forecourt area was filled with mountains of stores and equipment to supply the huge invasion force leaving Weymouth. Cross over to the side of the harbour, where you will see a sign for Sea Cruises. The Harbour Steps here, down to the water's edge, mark the final departure point for the American troops bound for Normandy. Picture the scene of bustle and clamour as men and their equipment were marshalled aboard a fleet of landing craft. They were packed into these vessels like sardines in cans (opposite) and when bad weather delayed the start of the invasion, they were forced to endure many extra hours in cramped and difficult conditions before their ordeal at Omaha began.

Here you can finish the first section of your walk with a stroll along the harbourside towards the Town Bridge. The area is always interesting, with fishing boats and various pleasure craft coming and going. You may see a tall ship or two, or even be able to watch the Weymouth Lifeboat preparing to answer an emergency call! The wartime lifeboat based here, *William and Clara Ryland*, took part in many rescue missions, including searching for pilots whose planes had ditched into the sea. A visit to the Lifeboat Museum Shop, on The Nothe side of the harbour, will tell you more of the long history of lifeboats here.

See www.weymouthlifeboat.org.uk for more information.

Men are packed into landing craft like sardines in cans and must endure their cramped conditions even longer as bad weather puts back the D-Day departure. (Courtesy Weymouth Museum)

WALK 2: THE NOTHE WALK

from the Town Bridge to Brewers Quay and The Nothe.

The Town Bridge over the harbour marks the starting point for the walk to The Nothe. Cross over the bridge and Holy Trinity Church will be before you. A large part of old Weymouth beyond this Church suffered some of the heaviest bombing that the town endured during the war.

Turn left along the harbourside, and within minutes you will be approaching the wartime base for *My Girl*, pinpointed by the Coastline Cruises Kiosk on the edge of the quay. The soldiers of the Royal Artillery Regiment, "The Gunners", assembled here to board the vessel for duties at the forts which guarded Portland Harbour and the Naval Base. Here, Ron Hill would board *My Girl*, preparing for another day's duties, conveying men and stores to the Portland Breakwater Forts (opposite). Other passengers included ENSA Concert Parties (great morale boosters during those dark days), and in 1942, American servicemen began to join their British counterparts.

In the summer months, *My Girl* and her companion vessel *Enchantress* await you here.

Don't miss an opportunity to return for a memorable voyage to Portland, or a cruise across the bay to Redcliff or Lulworth Cove, viewing the famous Jurassic Coastline. See www.coastlinecruises.com for more information.

Ron Hill aboard *My Girl* at Hope Quay, preparing for another day's duties conveying men and stores to the Portland Breakwater Forts. (Author's Collection)

Cross over to Cove Street, or Trinity Street, both of which will take you into Hope Square and Brewers Quay. This area has many opportunities for refreshment with a good choice of pubs, restaurants and little cafes, plus art galleries, a chandlery and some interesting houses from the Tudor era.

The Brewers Quay building presently houses a host of small antique and collectibles stalls, together with the Weymouth Museum. The museum occupies temporary galleries at this time, pending its relocation within this Victorian building when renovation work has been undertaken. The town has a rich vein of history ranging from Roman times, through the Tudor,

Civil War and Georgian eras, to the early twentieth century, and the museum holds a large collection of local artefacts. The impressive photographic collection stored there supplied many of the D-Day pictures for this book, as gratefully acknowledged. Ensure you visit this great local resource to find out more of Weymouth's fascinating history, and details of special events. See www.weymouthmuseum.org.uk for more information.

Follow the road along the front and side of the Brewers Quay building, to Horsford Street, which leads to Barrack Road and The Nothe Gardens and Fort. This is your gateway to some of the best views in all of Weymouth! Take in the Weymouth panorama near the parapet of the stone steps immediately adjacent to the first area of parking to your left. You can view Weymouth Harbour below, with the arc of the bay beyond, and the cliffs of the magnificent Jurassic Coastline.

Follow the central road through the gardens, passing other areas of parking, and the main gate of The Nothe Fort will be before you. The big guns of this historic building were used to guard the approaches to Weymouth Harbour and the bay in wartime. Plan a visit to The Nothe Fort Museum, which includes a cafeteria, for a great experience for adults and children, taking you through its history from Victorian times to the present day. The museum includes a Weymouth at War exhibit, and many special events are also held here throughout the year. Outside, from the ramparts of the fort, the sea views all around are breathtaking, and these waters, including Portland Harbour, provided the arena for the Olympic Sailing Events in 2012. See www.nothefort.org.uk for more information.

Home Guards at The Nothe, undertaking target practice with Lee-Enfield rifles. The shoreline of Weymouth Bay, visible in the background, was barricaded during the war years.
(Courtesy Nothe Fort Museum)

On leaving the fort, you can follow the paths for a stroll in the lovely south-facing gardens which lead down to the sea, with seating areas to enjoy the view, or retrace your steps back to Brewers Quay, the Harbourside and the Town Bridge.

WALK 3 - Castletown, Portland

Keen walkers can follow the road link or the coastal path from Weymouth to Portland, but there are various transport links available. You can travel by car or bus, including an open-top bus service which operates during the summer months. Another summertime travel link between Weymouth and Castletown is via the Coastline Cruises vessels *My Girl* and *Enchantress*, as already mentioned.

Your route by road from Weymouth to Portland takes you along the causeway which runs beside the famous Chesil Beach. This beach is an 18-mile long bank of pebbles stretching along the Dorset coast, with the sheltered waters of Portland Harbour to the east side, and the powerful seas of Lyme Bay to the west. The road crosses the entrance to the Fleet Lagoon at Ferrybridge, and The Chesil Beach Visitor Centre, developed over recent years, appears immediately on your right. The centre's extensive car park was originally created as part of the D-Day preparations for a marshalling area for tanks and vehicles awaiting loading onto tank landing craft at Castletown (opposite). The Visitor Centre has a good cafe/restaurant facility, and is very interesting and informative about the beach and the wildlife of the area. See www. dorsetwildlifetrust.org.uk/chesilbeach for more information

4/5 June 1944. Vehicles rumbled through Weymouth and headed for the marshalling area at Ferrybridge. When that was full, they parked nose to tail along the Chesil Beach Road.
(Courtesy Weymouth Museum)

The Portland Harbour vista on the left side of the road has changed dramatically during recent decades. The butterfly wings of sailboards, and little shoals of sailing dinghies now skim the waters where the largest warships of the Royal Navy previously anchored. Today, cruise liners and cable ships call at the commercial port which has replaced the Naval Dockyard. There is now a thriving marina with berths for many yachts, and, taking pride of place, is the National Sailing Academy, which hosted the sailing events of the 2012 Olympic Games. See www.wpnsa.org.uk for more information. The harbour is also a regular venue for the World Windspeed Championships, and many records have been set here.

On arrival by land at Portland, which is the home of the renowned Portland Stone used in many famous buildings including St. Paul's Cathedral in London – a symbol of wartime resistance –your route will take you past the Victoria Gardens, containing the island's own World War 2 Memorial to the American troops who left these shores. Follow the signs for Castletown and Portland Castle, and take the road past the tall blocks of former Naval accommodation which have begun their transformation into marine apartments, to the little beach backed by a small row of houses and shops.

As in Weymouth, imagine the world changing events taking place here in 1944, in the run up to D-Day. Preparations had to be hidden at times under vast clouds of smokescreens. The harbour was filled with ships. Tank landing craft approached this beach from the sea, one after the other, their jaws wide open to swallow the tanks and lorries which lined up to cross the Channel, along with troops and their equipment, to begin the liberation of Europe (opposite).

Just offshore, two sections of the huge concrete Mulberry Harbours, which were towed to France to form artificial harbours, still remain as a reminder of the part they played on the battlefront. The planned Heritage Centre for Castletown will, when completed, welcome visitors and feature all the history of the events which took place here.

4/5 June 1944. Loading landing craft; at Castletown, Portland.
The Harbour and Weymouth Bay beyond bristle with warships
which will bombard the French coast to soften up the enemy defences prior to the arrival of the invasion force.
(Courtesy Geoffrey Carter)

Walk back now to Portland Castle, on Liberty Road. Built in
the 1540s, as part of Henry VIII's coastal defences, the castle,
which housed military personnel during the war, allows you
to step back in time as you explore within its walls. English
Heritage often holds themed events here, and amenities
include a large car park, a cafe and a gift shop. See www.
english-heritage.org.uk for more information.

From the car park beside the castle, you can gain access to the
promenade on the harbour's edge. A short stroll takes you
to the National Sailing Academy and the marina. There are
opportunities here to take in the lovely harbour views, and

to relax and enjoy refreshments before retracing your steps back to Castletown. Walk 3 is now complete, but if you are willing to go an extra mile on the island, you will be rewarded with a coastal panorama which ranks as one of the finest in the whole of Britain. Follow the incline of the road from Castletown, through Fortuneswell, to the top of Portland, and to the War Memorial situated just beyond The Heights Hotel. The view from this point, which Ron Hill described in his walk in *The Clouds of War*, is truly spectacular.

To the west, Lyme Bay is bounded by the coastlines of Dorset and Devon, and this expanse of sea is majestic when sunlit and tranquil. However, when stormy conditions prevail, this scene is awesome as great waves thunder up to the top of the beach, flinging clouds of spray over the rooftop of the Cove Inn perched on the promenade at Chiswell. To the east of Chesil Beach, lies the Fleet Lagoon, and the causeway between Portland and Weymouth; the roadside areas here take on a soft pink hue each spring as thousands of sea thrift flowers come into bloom. Portland Harbour is a popular venue for sailboarders, paddle-boarders and kite-surfers, and flotillas of sailing dinghies from the National Sailing Academy can also be glimpsed skimming across its surface. Beyond the Breakwaters, Weymouth's beautiful bay is framed by the green hills and white cliffs of the Jurassic Coast.

Take time... to explore and experience the beauty of the sea and sky around you, to look a gull in the eye as it hangs in the air beside you, and to take a breath of air no other person has breathed before you... this is a special place. Remember sometimes, that your freedom to enjoy this coastline – and all of its gifts – was bought for you by the service and sacrifice of others.

Lightning Source UK Ltd.
Milton Keynes UK
UKOW06f0837240616

276982UK00003B/28/P

9 781910 819777